Quick & Clever
Felting

Ellen Kharade

Printed in China by SNP Leefung Pte Ltd
for David & Charles
Brunel House   Newton Abbot   Devon

3946
Executive Editor Cheryl Brown
Desk Editor Bethany Dymond
Art Editor Sarah Underhill
Designer Mia Farrant
Project Editors Jo Richardson and Betsy Hosegood
Production Controller Kelly Smith
Photographer Kim Sayer and Karl Adamson

Visit our website at www.davidandcharles.co.uk

David & Charles books are available from all good bookshops; alternatively, you
can contact our Orderline on 0870 9908222 or write to us at FREEPOST EX2
110, D&C Direct, Newton Abbot, TQ12 4ZZ (no stamp required UK only); US
customers call 800-289-0963 and Canadian customers call 800-840-5220.

Contents

Introduction

Felt fabric is such a beautiful, tactile fabric as well as being so easy to work with, and its special qualities can be enjoyed in many different handcrafted forms, from fun toys and eye-catching decorations to stylish accessories for the home and to wear.

My love of felting began when I decided to recycle a couple of unpromising ready-felted items. The first was a dull wool felt blanket, which I transformed by hand dying it a lovely turquoise colour and appliquéing it with large, brown leaves. The second was my favourite Fair Isle jumper, rendered unwearable through being accidentally shrunk in the washing machine, but in the process metamorphosed into a sturdy, jewel-like fabric, which I cut up and restyled to make a fabulous bag (see pages 34–39 for how to make your own version).

From then, it was a natural progression to create homemade felt fabric. The process of taking carded fleece and turning it into a dense, usable fabric is like alchemy, and opens up a whole new crafting world. This book offers an exciting exploration into this world, presenting a range of ways in which felt fabric can be created, decorated and applied for quick and clever projects. The simplest method uses ready-made synthetic felt in innovative ways and with interesting embellishments – see the Glittering Tree Decorations, page 26, where cutout motifs are backed with colourful voile and decorated with embroidery and beads, or the Mirrored Jewellery Boxes, page 82, which are covered with vibrantly coloured felt adorned with ornamental mirrors and sequins.

The technique of needle felting, where carded fleece is repeatedly stabbed with barbed needles to interlock it with the base fabric, can be used to add decorative details, as on the Denim and Daisy Elephant, page 30, or to produce three-

For really quick results, use ready-made felt and combine it with other fabrics as required. These festive tree decorations are cut from glitter felt (see page 26).

Did you know that you can needle felt onto other fabrics? Make this pretty, cuddly toy elephant from soft denim to see how it's done (see page 30).

dimensional items, either simply worked over polystyrene formers, as for the Springtime Egg Hangings, page 56, or built up in layers, as in the Beautiful Bird Mobile, page 46.

Some of the projects exploit the striking colour effects that can be achieved by using dyed felt fabric – see the Vibrant Document Bag, page 62, where the cerise-dyed front flap features a cutout design silhouetted against contrasting-coloured felt. Other projects employ the technique of wet felting, where carded fleece is wetted and rubbed with soap, then rolled in a bamboo blind to harden and shrink the fibres, resulting in a soft, warm and durable fabric. The ingenious applications of this method shown in the book include creating a built-in pattern, as used for the luxurious Christmas stocking, page 72, wet felting

around a plastic template to create a seamless three-dimensional shape, as for the christening booties, page 98, and forming beads of wet-felted fleece to make a novel necklace (see page 68) or simply to use as decoration, as in the Jester-Style Slippers, page 112.

Most of the projects can be easily completed within a day, and many include variations on the basic design to encourage your own creativity. Felting is a little like cooking, and once you become more familiar with its ingredients and methods, you will want to make your own changes and adaptations or discover your own clever tricks and shortcuts. So use these quick and clever felting ideas as a framework for developing your own methods and expertise.

You can easily needle felt around a polystyrene former to create beautiful felted shapes in no time, like these super eggs (see page 56). Detailing is added with further needle felting or by gluing or pinning on embellishments.

Wet felting around a plastic or foil template enables you to make seamless forms, like these delightful christening booties (see page 98).

Materials

Here is a quick guide to the types of felt you can buy ready to use as well as the raw material you need to make your own homemade felt fabric (see pages 10–18). And for those who are keen to recycle old or discarded items, instructions are given for felting woollens in the washing machine or dying wool felt fabric, such as old blankets, to create totally revamped felt to use in all the different ways explored in this book.

Ready-made felt

Manufactured felt is made from synthetic fibres and comes in an array of vivid colours. It is available in small squares (usually 25cm/10in) or off the roll. As with other kinds of felt, it doesn't fray, but because synthetic felt is thin, it isn't as hard wearing as hand-felted or handmade wool felt fabric. On the positive side, its thinness means that it is malleable and therefore ideal for curving around boxes, as in the Mirrored Jewellery Boxes, page 82, or soft enough to fold around books to cover them, as in the Star Notebook Cover, page 22. Synthetic felt is also available in 5mm (¼in) thick squares, but not off the roll and the colours can be limited.

Nepal wool is a hand-felted fabric from India. It is a thick felt with densely packed fibres, which makes it durable and hard wearing. It comes in a variety of colours but in a limited size, in rectangles measuring 30 x 42cm (12 x 16½in), so is therefore only suitable for fairly small projects – see the Vibrant Document Bag, page 62, for example, where it is used as a colourful backdrop for a cutaway design.

Carded fleece

This is the raw material used for both needle felting (see page 10) and wet felting (see page 14). You will see carded fleece sold as wool tops, but it is also known as carded wool or combed tops, and is simply referred to as 'fleece' in the instructions in the book. You can make felt out of most animal fibres, including llama and angora, and there are many different types of wool on the market for you to try as you get more adventurous. However, sheep's wool remains the most widely available and the variety used in the book is Merino from the Merino sheep, which is good quality and felts extremely well due to its fine, short fibres (see Suppliers, page 127). The wool is cleaned and then combed (carded) before being sold as wool tops. It comes in long lengths, usually in 50g or 100g bags (1¾oz or 3½oz).

Carded fleece is available in a wonderfully wide variety of colours. Take advantage of this and pick your favourites for the projects in this book.

Manufactured synthetic felt is available in a range of bright colours off the roll as well as in 25cm (10in) squares, which are ideal for making small items.

Angelina fibres

These are very fine synthetic fibres that reflect and refract the light to create iridescent and luminescent highlights. They come in a huge range of colours and can be easily incorporated into carded fleece during the felting process – see pages 112–115 where they add an extra sparkle to the Jester-Style Slippers.

Machine-washed woollens

Machine- or hand-knitted garments can be felted in the washing machine very successfully. The item to be felted must be more than 80 per cent wool for the felting process to work properly. Place the woollen garment in the washing machine with a pair of old jeans (the friction helps to speed up the felting process) and put on a 60°C (140°F) wash cycle with ordinary detergent. Once the felt has dried, it is ready to be cut up and used, as in the Favourite Jumper Bag, page 34.

Quick and clever hand dying

1 Hand wash the felt fabric with soap flakes or a detergent for woollens to remove any dirt and stains, then squeeze out the excess water and leave it damp.

2 Fill a bowl with enough cold water to cover the fabric.

3 Dissolve the dye in 500ml (1 pint) of hot tap water and add to the bowl.

4 Add 375ml (13fl oz) of white vinegar to the dye bath and stir well until all the dye has dissolved.

5 Add the fabric to the dye bath, stirring constantly for the first ten minutes and lifting the fabric out of the dye and unfolding it to prevent any creases from forming.

6 Once the fabric has taken on the dye to the desired shade, rinse it in cold water until the water runs clear, spin the fabric on a wool cycle and leave in a warm place to dry out.

Dyed wool felt fabric

Natural-coloured wool felt fabric can be easily dyed using cold-water hand dyes or machine dyes to match or coordinate with any colour scheme. Modern synthetic dyes come in almost every colour imaginable and are intermixable. They are also light stable, which means that the colours are less likely to fade over time. In this way, old wool blankets can be transformed into beautifully coloured felt fabric ready to be made up into cushions (see the Quick Appliqué Cushion, page 106), bags (see the Vibrant Document Bag, page 62) and other attractive items. Hand dying is ideal for dying smaller items, whereas larger pieces can be dyed quite successfully in the washing machine. Note that the colour and texture of woollen fabric dyed in the machine will be different from that of hand-dyed fabric because of the felting that occurs in the process.

You can dye felt fabric to achieve strongly contrasting colours or coordinating shades of a particular colour palette, depending on the application – see, for example, the Tropical and Snowflake Tote Bags, pages 86–91, one in citrus shades, the other in cool pastels.

General Equipment and Techniques

These pages focus on the routine equipment and basic techniques needed for making up the projects in this book. The more specialist techniques and their related equipment, such as needle felting and wet felting, are covered in the subsequent pages of this section.

Scissors

It is a good idea to keep a variety of scissors as a part of your general tool kit. Always use them for the job for which they were intended and never leave them lying around where they can be damaged or misused. Respect your scissors and always return them to their designated place after use.

Pinking shears

These are a good way of finishing off work without the need for hemming. They can also be used to create a decorative edging to fabric, such as the circles that form the rosette for the Star Notebook Cover, page 22.

General-purpose scissors

As their name indicates, these scissors are designed to cut most materials, such as paper, card and fabric, as well as thin plastic, which is used for the templates of the Christening Booties, page 102, and the Jester-Style Slippers, page 112.

Dressmaking scissors

These scissors have large cutting blades and are ideal for cutting big pieces of fabric or larger shapes from templates with ease.

Embroidery scissors

With their small pointed blades, these scissors are normally used for cutting threads, but they are also invaluable for cutting out intricate shapes, such as the pineapple motifs for the Tropical Tote Bag, page 86, or the design for the Vibrant Document Bag, page 62.

Adhesives

There are many different kinds of adhesive on the market, and you need to make the appropriate choice according to the type of gluing task you are carrying out.

PVA (white) glue

This is a water-based adhesive that can be used to glue most lightweight materials, such as paper, wood, fabric, sequins and beads. It has very good bonding properties but dries to a relatively rigid finish, so it is not always suitable for fabric. If in doubt, carry out a small test patch first. In the Mirrored Jewellery Boxes, page 82, it is used for gluing on all the embellishments, including shisha mirrors and different kinds of sequins (see also page 19).

Fabric glue

This adhesive is similar to PVA (white) glue but is less rigid once dry, although the bonding properties are the same. The cutout design for the Vibrant Document Bag, page 62, and the pineapple and snowflake motifs for the Tote Bags, pages 86–91, have all been stuck on using fabric glue.

Epoxy resin

The two parts of this solvent-based adhesive must be mixed together for the glue to be activated. It has very strong bonding properties and is suitable for sticking china, glass and wood, as in the Christening Rattle, page 98, where it is used to glue the length of wood dowel to polystyrene balls.

Sewing kit

Over time, you will build up a sewing kit that is very personal to you and will contain your favourite items, but the following is a list of the tools and materials that are essential for basic machine and hand sewing, and many of these items are needed for every project in the book, so therefore are not itemized again in the 'You will need' lists for each specific project.

- Tape measure
- A variety of marker pens, including a fade-away marker pen and chalk pencils in various colours
- Dressmaker's pins
- A variety of scissors (see opposite)
- Needles for hand sewing
- Medium gauge sewing machine needles
- Sewing threads in a variety of colours, including special-effect threads such as metallics

Using bonding web

Bonding web provides a quick and clever way of joining pieces of fabric together permanently, as in the Star Notebook Cover, page 22, where it is used to fuse three different-sized circles of felt together to create a rosette embellishment. It is especially invaluable when appliquéing a more intricate, multi-piece design onto fabric, as in the Quick Appliqué Cushion, page 106.

1 Using a hot iron, iron the bonding web onto the back of the fabric you plan to use for your motif. Pin the template to the front of the backed fabric and carefully cut out the shape or shapes.

2 Peel away the backing paper, position the motif(s) in place on the base fabric and press down with the hot iron to bond the motif(s) in position.

Quick and clever machine stitching

Sewing felt together with a sewing machine couldn't be easier because felt doesn't slip, it doesn't slide and it doesn't fray. However, it can be relatively bulky to sew through and may cause a problem. To address this, regulate the pressure-foot gauge on your sewing machine to accommodate thicker fabrics. This lever is frequently situated at the top of the machine, but do check its position with your manufacturer's handbook. For very bulky areas, where two or more pieces of felt intersect, set the pressure-foot gauge at zero, lift the foot and 'free sew' over the area.

Tip
A blunt machine needle will drag through your felt and may snag it, so remember to change yours regularly.

Quick and clever slipstitching

Slipstitch is especially useful for sewing linings into bags, as in the Tropical Tote Bag, page 86, and working 'invisible' slipstitches will give a truly professional finish. Pin the layers you wish to stitch together. Thread a small needle with matching thread and secure the thread out of sight – under a fabric fold if possible – with a few small stitches. Bring the needle out on one side of the join or hem and then pick up a small amount of fabric/felt on the other side. Insert the needle back on the first side and slip the needle along the fold or under the fabric, bringing it out a little way further on to make the next stitch.

Needle Felting

Needle felting is a way of felting fabric by repeatedly stabbing dry carded fleece into a base fabric using a very sharp barbed needle, thereby interlocking the fibres until they bond together. In addition to wool felt fabric, other fabrics can be used as a base for needle felting, such as cotton (see the Denim and Daisy Elephant, page 30) and linen. Fleece can also be needle felted onto polystyrene formers, as for the Springtime Egg Hangings, page 56, or hand moulded to create more free-flowing forms, as in the Beautiful Bird Mobile, page 46. Very fine detail, such as facial features or small areas of a different colour, can be worked into the needle-felted form with ease and accuracy using a single felting needle.

Equipment

- Felting needles – medium gauge for covering larger areas; fine gauge for small details, such as features
- Multi-needle felting tool – a wooden-handled tool that can hold up to four felting needles at one time, for needle felting over large areas; again, choose medium gauge for the largest areas and small gauge where a more delicate application is required
- Good-quality carded fleece in a variety of different colours (see page 6)
- Foam block – essential for working over, to protect yourself and your work surface from the extremely sharp needles
- Additional items that you will need for specific projects might include polystyrene formers and chalk or fade-away markers

Tip
Always store felting needles in a case, not only for your safety, but because these needles break easily

Working a motif

Always keep the needle perpendicular when needle felting to avoid it breaking and keep your hands behind the tool to avoid accidents. Once you have finished working with the needles, always put them safely away and never leave them lying around where children can get hold of them. Dispose of broken needles by carefully wrapping them up in wads of newspaper.

1 Using a suitable marker, such as a pale-coloured chalk pencil for a dark fabric or a fine black marker or fade-away marker on paler fabrics, draw the motif to be needle felted onto the base fabric, either freehand or using a template as a guide.

2 Place a foam block under your work. Wrap the fleece around your finger to form a loop, then place the loop over one area of the motif, following the shape of the motif.

3 Using a medium-gauge felting needle, begin to stab the needle repeatedly through the fleece into the base fabric until the fleece fibres are locked into the fabric beneath.

4 Continue in the same way, following the marked outlines, until the whole motif has been filled in.

5 Test the completed needle-felted motif by gently pushing the wool – it should be firmly attached to the base fabric, and fairly flat and even, as shown.

Working a line or outline

Needle felting is ideal for creating patterns made up of or incorporating fine lines, whether straight or curved, or for outlining motifs – forms of embellishment that would be impossible to achieve using the wet-felting technique.

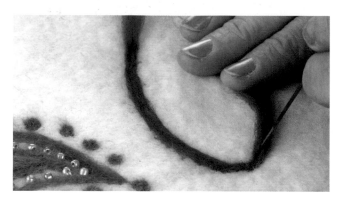

Using a suitable marker (see Step 1 on page 11), draw the outline or line to be needle felted, either freehand or using a template as a guide. Place a foam block under your work. Pull off a long, thin strand of fleece about 6mm (¼in) wide. Beginning at one end of the line or at a suitable point on the outline, stab the fleece into the base fabric with a medium- or fine-gauge felting needle, depending on the thickness of the line or outline, until it holds. Stab the thin strand repeatedly, following the shape of the marked line or outline, until it becomes a part of the base fabric beneath. Continue in the same way until the line or outline has been completely needle felted.

Working polka dots

Polka dots can introduce a colour change without being too overpowering or dominant. They are quick and easy to work using a medium- or fine-gauge felting needle, and have the same visual effect as using beads.

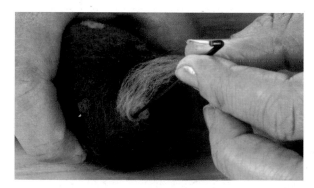

Pull off a very small tuft of fleece and position it on the base felt or fabric. Stab it repeatedly with the felting needle until the fleece locks together with the base fabric. Work in a small circle, stabbing the fleece repeatedly until it forms a dot about 3mm (⅛in) in diameter. Continue working the polka dot in circular, stabbing movements until it has increased to the desired size.

Working a solid shape

Solid shapes can be needle felted in small blocks using a medium-gauge felting needle. Sections of other colours can also be worked into the same area, building up a pattern at the same time.

Using a suitable marker (see Step 1 on page 11), draw the shape to be needle felted, either freehand or using a template as a guide. Place a foam block under your work. Pull off a tuft of fleece and lay it over the shape. Stab the fleece repeatedly until it no longer moves, following the shape, and continue stabbing until it becomes a part of the base fabric and the shape has been filled in. If working a different-coloured area around or adjacent to the shape, change fleece colour and continue needle felting in the same way, using a fine-gauge felting needle if it is a very small area.

Building up colour onto colour

As well as allowing you to lay a different-coloured shape adjacent to or around a solid needle-felted shape, you can work a different-coloured area directly on top of the needle-felted shape in a highly controlled way.

Place your work over a large foam block. Following a template as a reference if necessary, pull off a tuft of the fleece colour that you want to work over the solid needle-felted area. Starting at the thickest part of the needle-felted shape, lay the fleece down directly onto the surface. Stab the fleece repeatedly with the felting needle until it locks into the base fabric, and continue stabbing the fleece, following the shape that you want to add.

Creating a solid moulded shape

Fleece can be hand shaped and moulded to create a three-dimensional form using felting needles. This shape can then be further embellished with other colours – see opposite.

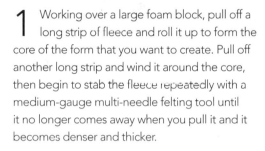

2 Add bulk to the form by continuing to wrap thin strips of fleece around it and needle felting to make it denser and more compact. Continue shaping the form by pinching and moulding it with your fingers.

1 Working over a large foam block, pull off a long strip of fleece and roll it up to form the core of the form that you want to create. Pull off another long strip and wind it around the core, then begin to stab the fleece repeatedly with a medium-gauge multi-needle felting tool until it no longer comes away when you pull it and it becomes denser and thicker.

3 Check the shape of the form against a template to see whether it is progressing in the way that you want. If not, add more fleece and continue stabbing with the felting needle, giving more shape to the areas that require it.

Needle felting around a former

Polystyrene formers provide ideal bases on which to build up needle felting very quickly, while at the same maintaining their perfect shape without fear of distortion. A multi-needle felting tool is ideal for covering formers efficiently and speedily.

2 Using a multi-needle felting tool, repeatedly stab the fleece strip into the polystyrene former so that it no longer comes away when you gently pull it. Turn the shape around and continue stabbing until the section you are working on has been covered. Pull off another strip of fleece the same size as before and needle felt it around the former in the same way. Continue until the former is completely covered and the felt has thickened. Any thin areas can be needle felted with wisps of fleece.

1 Pull off a long, relatively wide strip of fleece and wrap it around the polystyrene former.

Wet Felting

This technique enables you to make your own durable felt fabric in a wide variety of colours. Carded fleece is wetted and rubbed with soap to swell the scales on the shafts of the fibres, locking them together permanently, then the fleece is rolled in a bamboo blind or mat, causing further friction in what is known as the 'fulling' process, which thickens, hardens and shrinks the fibres. Not only plain but patterned fabric can be made by this method, and wet felting can also be used to create colourful felt balls, which make fun or decorative trimmings or beads.

Equipment

- Plastic mat – for protecting your work surface from splashing water and stray fibres
- Good-quality carded fleece in a variety of different colours (see page 6)
- Piece of net curtain – essential for covering your work before wetting and rubbing, as it keeps the fibres in one place
- Bowl of hand-hot water or a water spray bottle for wetting the fleece
- Bar of soap – any kind will do; its alkalinity speeds up the felting process
- Bamboo blind and mats – working directly on the blind creates the large amount of friction needed for felting to occur, and also makes transporting the work easier; small mats are useful for felting smaller-scale projects.
- Cotton cord or string – for tying up the ends of the blind prior to the rolling process
- Kettle and rubber gloves – for shocking the felt and to protect your hands during the process
- Old towels – for removing the excess water from the finished felt
- Cloths and bowl – for mopping up any excess water

Tip
Wet felting is more effective if you lay down several thin layers of fleece rather than a few thick layers.

Making one-colour felt

Always use thin tufts of fleece – the fibres won't felt sufficiently if you apply it in thick wads. When wetting and soaping, the more rubbing you do, the quicker the fleece will felt. The precise length of time it will take to roll or 'full' the fleece depends on a lot of factors, such as pressure, friction and heat, so you will have to judge by eye when the fabric has properly felted. Once you have created your first piece of felt, you will quickly be able to gauge how much fleece to put down and how much water to use.

1 Cover your work surface with a plastic mat, then lay the bamboo blind on top. Begin by cutting off sections of fleece roughly 10cm (4in) long, or slightly shorter if the project is on a small scale. Start by pulling a section of fleece until a large tuft comes away in your hand. Lay the fleece in one corner vertically, then lay down another tuft, slightly overlapping it. Continue to build up overlapping rows of fleece.

2 Pull off tufts of fleece and lay them down over the first row horizontally, starting in the corner. Continue as before, building up the layers gradually. Place a third layer of tufts down, this time laying them vertically. Check that there are no gaps in between the tufts of fleece and that the bamboo blind cannot be seen beneath. If any areas look thin, now is the time to fill them in.

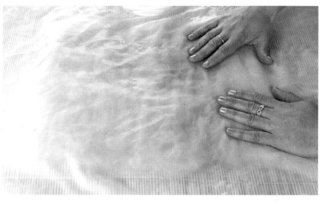

3 Lay a piece of net curtain over the fleece large enough to cover your work. Using hand-hot water, wet the fleece, either with a water spray or just by sprinkling water over. Make sure that the entire area is thoroughly wet but not sopping.

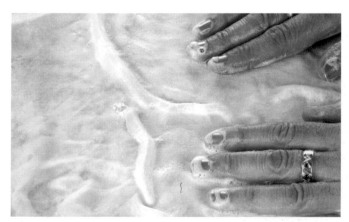

4 Rub the bar of soap over the entire surface. Use the flats of your hands to exert a little pressure, without disturbing the fleece beneath. Keep rubbing over the surface for at least 15 minutes until the fibres no longer move and the felt has meshed together. Turn the felt over and check the fibres, then repeat the rubbing process if they appear not as dense as on the other side.

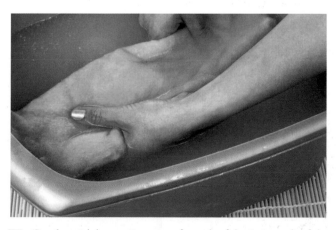

5 Gently peel the netting away from the felt. Agitate the felt in warm water to remove the soap. At this stage, the felt should be in one piece, but it is still very delicate, so handle it with care. Gently squeeze out any excess water.

Making one-colour felt cont...

6 Lay the felt at one end of the blind and roll it up as tightly as you can. Now tie a piece of cord or string at each end of the blind to keep it from unravelling during the rolling process.

7 With both hands, start rolling the blind backwards and forwards for at least ten minutes. Turn the fabric 90 degrees and continue rolling until you have moved through a 360-degree rotation. Periodically check the progress of the felt. Shock the felt by dunking it into hot water and then immediately into cold water. Roll again for another ten minutes until the felt has sufficiently thickened and hardened to the desired size. Finally, rinse the felt in warm water and roll it in towels to remove the excess. Leave overnight on the back of a chair in a warm room to dry out.

Making wet-felted balls

Balls can be formed from fleece using the wet-felting technique by wrapping it around a core and building up the shape gradually. Different sizes of balls can be produced in this way and varying colours added during the layering process to achieve interesting effects. The balls can be used for a fun trimming, as in the Jester-Style Slippers, page 112, as beads – see the Collar Necklace, page 68, or simply for decoration, as on the Vibrant Document Bag, page 62.

1 Pull off a length of fleece about 10cm (4in) long. Wet the strand with hand-hot water, rub a little soap over it and roll it up into a ball.

2 Pull off another strip of fleece about the same length and cover the ball, this time laying the fleece across it in the opposite direction. There is no need to wet this layer, as enough water will be transferred from the previous layer.

3 Start rolling the ball very gently in the palm of your hands until the shape is more ball-like. Continue rolling for about five minutes until the ball begins to feel denser and harder.

4 Cover the ball with finer strips of fleece, building up the size and rolling it gently in soapy hands to maintain the shape and felt the fibres.

5 Add more strips to build up the ball to the desired size. Any areas that look uneven can be covered with very fine wisps of fleece and rolled in your hands as before.

6 Once the ball has hardened slightly and you are happy with the size (note that it will shrink by a further 20%), roll it gently on a bamboo mat until it hardens and shrinks. Shock the ball in hot and then cold water, rinse out the soap thoroughly and leave in a warm place to dry.

Making patterned felt

It is easy and fun to create a pattern during the wet-felting process. The following instructions show how to make the diamond-patterned felt fabric used in A Stockingful of Sparkle, pages 72–75, complete with a plain red strip for the stocking top. Use this method to create other patterned felt too, such as tartans, checks and polka dots, which can then be made up into a variety of items, such as a teapot cosy, cushion, bag or even a themed wall hanging.

1 Lay down tufts of purple fleece vertically onto a large bamboo blind to cover an area about 80 x 100cm (32 x 40in), then tufts of red fleece over an area 80 x 20cm (32 x 8in) at one end, overlapping the purple fleece by at least 2cm (¾in), as in Step 1, page 15. (The finished fabric will be about 30% smaller all round.) Then add a horizontal and a final vertical layer, as in Step 2, page 15. Cut a length of red fleece long enough to span the work diagonally. Gently pull off a strand measuring about 1cm (⅜in) wide. Lay it diagonally across the centre of the work. Repeat to lay parallel strands across the fleece, keeping them evenly spaced.

2 Repeat the process to lay a length of darker red fleece beside each paler red strand. Now lay paler red strands in the diagonally opposite direction to complete the pattern. Adjust the strands if they have shifted in position.

Tip
To speed up the drying time, put the felt in the washing machine and spin it on a wool cycle before leaving it to dry.

3 Felt the fleece as in Steps 3 and 4 on page 15, starting in one corner – it will take at least 15–20 minutes for the fibres to bond together. Lift up the netting and check your work periodically, adjusting the pattern by pulling the fibres back into place. Once the fibres no longer stick to the netting, they have bonded enough to start the shrinking and hardening process.

4 Follow Steps 5–7 on pages 15–16 to complete the wet-felting process, carefully folding the felt up before rinsing it in hot water. After rolling or 'fulling' for 15 minutes, unroll the felt and turn it, then repeat the process until the felt has been rolled in all directions. This ensures that it shrinks evenly.

Making a hollow shape

Wet felting can be worked around a former to create a hollow shape. Plastic and foil formers both work very well as barriers to stop the fibres from meshing together; cardboard tubes, for instance, can be covered in foil. In the following case, a tube shape is made using a foil former, to create the trumpet for the Daffodil Corsage, pages 96–97.

1 Wrap some wisps of fleece around your finger until it is covered. Wet with warm water and rub gently until the fibres no longer move around. Build up the layers with thin strips of fleece. Gently ease the tube off your finger and cover the end with some more wisps of fleece. Wet, soap and rub as before until the fibres no longer move.

2 Rinse the felt in water. Place a piece of scrunched-up foil in the fleece tube and roll it up in a bamboo mat. Roll backwards and forwards until the fleece has thickened. Shock the fleece in hot and then cold water and repeat the rolling process until the felt tube has felted and shrunk to the desired size.

Making an all-in-one bootie

Plastic sheeting is another good barrier to felt directly onto, as it is flexible and easily cut to shape. Although the plastic is two dimensional, you can use it to create a variety of three-dimensional forms, such as booties and slippers – see the Christening Booties, page 98, and the Jester-Style Slippers, page 112. The Christening Booties are particularly clever as both booties are made at one time using a double-ended plastic template, which, once felted, is snipped down the centre into two separate pieces. The same method could be used on a larger scale to make other seamless three-dimensional objects, such as bags and bowls.

1 Cut your shape from paper. Lay the paper template over the sheet of plastic and secure in place with adhesive tape. Using a marker, carefully draw around the template onto the plastic, then accurately cut out, keeping as close to the pen marks as possible.

2 Lay the plastic template on the bamboo blind. Pull pieces of fleece into tufts and lay them vertically across the template, overlapping one row over the other and the sides of the template. Once the fleece has been wetted, soaped and rubbed, turn the template over and fold in the edges of wet felt to create the seamless shape. Continue following the instructions on pages 15–16, applying three layers to both sides, one vertical, one horizontal and one vertical, overlapping and folding in the first two layers; there is no need to overlap the final layer.

Embellishments

Buttons, beads, sequins and embroidery (see pages 20–21) can give your felted projects additional colour, texture and sparkle, or look out for shisha mirrors, which look wonderfully exotic (see the Mirrored Jewellery Boxes, page 82). Buttons, beads and sequins can be stitched to the felt as explained here, or you can glue or pin them in place, if preferred.

Beads can be threaded onto embroidery cotton (floss) in the process of embroidering (see the Tropical Tote Bag, page 86) or stitched on with thread, as on the needle-felted egg cosy, page 81. Both beads and buttons should be sewn on with a double length of thread and knotted before and after they are worked to ensure that they don't come off.

Store your embellishments by type in transparent glass or plastic containers for easy selection – they also make an attractive display!

Sequins can be used like beads. When sewing onto felt fabric or wet-felted balls (see pages 68–71), bring the needle and thread up through the centre of the sequin and sew in place before finishing off by threading the needle back through the centre of the sequin again. Secure the thread with a knot before and after the sequin has been worked.

Tip
Some sequins don't have a pre-formed hole in the centre, but you can make a hole by placing a nail on the sequin and gently tapping it with a hammer.

Embroidery

You don't need to be an expert with a needle and thread to try the simple embroidery stitches used for the projects in this book. Even simple stitches such as running stitch or flower stitch look great, and a few uneven stitches will simply add to the handcrafted look.

Embroidery cotton (floss)

This comes in skeins comprised of six fine strands of thread that can be worked together for a bold effect, or separated into fewer strands to create finer stitches. The skeins are available in a rainbow of colours as well as different finishes: plain, multi-coloured or metallic.

Embroidery stitches

Several different traditional embroidery stitches have been used to embellish the projects in this book, from a simple running stitch to the fancier lazy-daisy stitch.

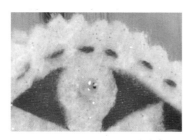

Running stitch

This simplest of stitches, commonly used to attach two pieces of fabric together, can also be used decoratively, especially for outlining a motif, sewn in a contrasting thread colour. Working from right to left, simply pass the needle in and out of the fabric, making several stitches at a time and keeping their length even.

Backstitch

This stitch is worked to create a continuous line of stitching, and can be used to add linear details to motifs, such as veins for leaves. Working from right to left, make a stitch as for running stitch, bringing the needle out one stitch length away. Now insert the needle at the end of the first stitch and bring it out two stitch lengths away.

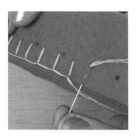

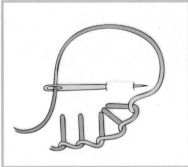

Blanket stitch

Use blanket stitch to create a decorative edging, perhaps worked in a contrasting thread colour. Working from left to right, insert the needle into the fabric a little way from the edge, the distance depending on the size of stitches you want to make, leaving the loose end of thread running down over the edge at right angles to it. Take the threaded end over the loose end and insert the needle a little way along at the same distance from the edge as before, then pass the needle through the loop of thread and gently pull up the thread.

Star stitch

Often used as a centre for flowers, this decorative stitch can be worked on a very small scale. Push the needle up through the front of the fabric and down through it to create a stitch about 5mm (¼in) long, then bring the needle out to one side to make a stitch over the first one, forming a cross. Continue to work the other diagonals in the same way until you have a star with eight points. Long star stitch is worked in the same way, but the lengths of the stitches are varied.

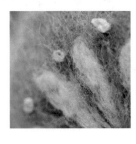

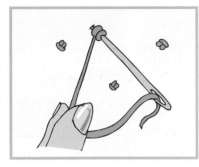

French knot

This neat little knot can be worked singly, or close together to cover a whole area. Bring the needle through to the front of the fabric. With the thread held taut, twist the needle twice around the thread. Pull the thread to tighten the twists a little, then keeping the thread taut, insert the needle back into the fabric close to the exit point. Pull the needle through the twists to the back of the fabric.

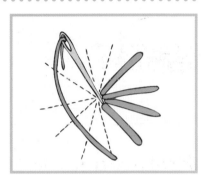

Flower stitch

Flower stitch looks similar to star stitch but is worked from the outer points into the centre, and can also be stitched on a larger scale. Start with the thread emerging from the tip of one of the points, then insert the needle down through the centre of the flower and bring it out at the tip of the next point round.

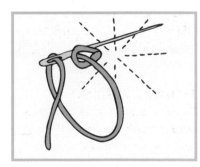

Lazy-daisy stitch

This dainty little flower stitch is worked in a similar way to chain stitch. With the thread emerging near the centre of the flower, insert the needle next to the emerging thread and bring it out at the tip of one of the points, passing it through the loop of thread. Pull the thread so that the loop lies flat, then anchor the loop with a small, straight stitch, bringing the needle out near the centre of the flower ready to form the next petal.

Star Notebook Cover

This handsome little jacket will bring a touch of distinction to any notebook, and makes a charming gift, perhaps to celebrate a specific achievement, such as passing an exam or test. Its design is simplicity itself and involves minimal sewing: the ends of a long rectangle of felt are folded in and sewn to the inside so that the notebook can be simply slipped into it. The decorative felt rosette and band are easily constructed and attached with iron-on bonding web, while embroidered stars and a little sequin and bead detailing add a fun finishing touch.

Iron-on bonding web is used to bond the black felt band to the centre of the white felt cover and to layer the three felt circles that create the smart rosette.

Pretty stars are worked in red embroidery cotton (floss) in a vertical row either side of the rosette band.

A single red sequin is sewn to the centre of the rosette, topped with a tiny gold bead, to add a final embellishment.

You will need

- 1 notebook • White synthetic felt, enough to cover your notebook, plus a little extra for the rosette (see Steps 1–2) • Scrap of synthetic red felt • Black synthetic felt, 25cm (10in) square • Bonding web, about 30cm (12in) square • 1 skein of red embroidery cotton (floss) • 1 small red sequin • 1 tiny gold bead • Set square • Iron • Compass • Sewing kit (see page 9)

1 Open out the notebook you want to make the cover for and place it cover-side up on your work surface. Measure the height and length of the book and add 8cm (3¼in) to the length. Using a set square and a fade-away marker, measure and mark out a rectangle of those dimensions on the white felt.

2 Using a hot iron, press the bonding web onto some white and red felt and the square of black felt (see page 9). Using a compass, draw a 6cm (2½in), 5cm (2in) and 3.5cm (1½in) diameter circle on paper to make templates. Pin the smallest circle to the white felt and cut out with pinking shears. Use the middle-sized template to cut a black felt circle and the largest template to cut a red felt circle. Cut a 3cm (1¼in) strip of black felt the same length as the height of the white felt cover.

Tip
Save your paper templates – you never know when you might need them again (see the bookmark opposite, for example).

3 Peel away the backing paper from the bonding web on the reverse of the black felt strip and iron it onto the front cover of the jacket, making sure that it is central – there is an extra 4cm (1⅝in) fold-over allowance on the right-hand edge, so you need to take this into account. Arrange the three circles for the rosette and iron them in place, making sure that they are sitting centrally on the black strip.

4 Using the fade-away marker, draw a series of dots on either side of the central motif, keeping them evenly spaced. Thread a needle with three strands of red embroidery cotton (floss) and work neat little star stitches (see page 21) over each of the marks.

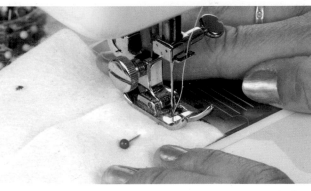

6 Fold 4cm (1⅝in) to the inside of the back of the cover and pin the top and bottom edges together; machine stitch in place. Repeat for the front of the cover.

5 Thread a needle with a double length of white thread and knot the end. Sew a red sequin topped with a gold bead in the centre of the rosette and then knot the thread on the back to finish.

Matching Bookmark

Why not make an elegant bookmark using leftover pieces of felt and present it with a book – possibly even your covered notebook – as a personalized gift? You could make a few of them, varying the colour scheme.

Using pinking shears, cut out a strip of black felt 21.5 x 5.5cm (8½ x 2¼in). Iron a strip of bonding web onto the back of a piece of red felt (see page 9) and cut out a 19 x 3cm (7½ x 1¼in) strip. Iron a square of bonding web onto the back of a piece of white felt. Using a 3.5cm (1½in) diameter paper template, cut out a series of four circles from the white felt with the pinking shears. Iron the red strip onto the black strip and then iron each circle onto the red strip at evenly spaced intervals. Thread a needle with three strands of red embroidery cotton (floss) and embroider a star stitch in the centre of each circle (see page 21). Use a hole punch to make a hole at the top of the bookmark and thread with a length of narrow red ribbon.

Glittering Tree Decorations

Nothing is more fun than getting into the Christmas spirit by handcrafting decorations for the tree, and these favourite festive motifs are guaranteed to delight everyone. Children will love making their own special versions and bringing them out year after year. Each decoration has been made from two layers of synthetic glitter felt with coloured voile sandwiched in between, to create an alluring combination of shimmering textures. The layers are simply glued together for a fast finish, and embellished with an easy running stitch and dainty beads and sequins.

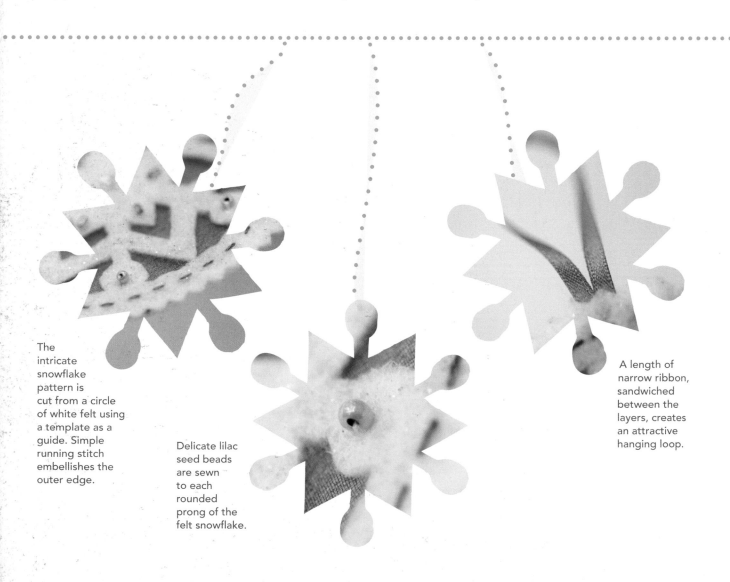

The intricate snowflake pattern is cut from a circle of white felt using a template as a guide. Simple running stitch embellishes the outer edge.

Delicate lilac seed beads are sewn to each rounded prong of the felt snowflake.

A length of narrow ribbon, sandwiched between the layers, creates an attractive hanging loop.

You will need

- Synthetic felt, 25cm (10in) square – glitter white, glitter blue, mid blue and lilac • Scraps of voile – purple and blue • 1 skein each of six-stranded embroidery cotton (floss) – lilac, blue, mint and white • Seed beads – lilac and mint • Silver glass rocaille beads • Decorative sequins • About 10 small pearl beads for the tree design • Narrow ribbon – lilac, blue, pale blue and mint green • PVA (white) glue • Compass • Sewing kit (see page 9)

1 Using a compass, draw an 8.5cm (3½in) diameter circle onto scrap paper and cut out. Pin the circle template to the white felt. Using pinking shears, cut around the circle twice to make two matching circles.

Tip
Coordinate your designs with the overall colour scheme of your tree. For a Scandinavian feel, red and white would look very effective interspersed between swags of popcorn and cranberries.

2 Using the template on page 116, cut out a snowflake from paper. Pin the snowflake to one of the white felt circles. Carefully cut out the inner areas of the design with embroidery scissors. Now pin the circle template to the purple voile and cut out with the pinking shears.

3 Thread a needle with three strands of lilac embroidery cotton (floss) and work running stitches around the outer edge of the white felt snowflake (see page 20), keeping the stitches neat and even. Use a double length of white thread to sew a lilac seed bead onto each rounded prong of the snowflake. Sew a silver rocaille bead onto each inner point of the snowflake and then stick a sequin in the centre with a dot of PVA (white) glue.

4 Form a loop from a 15cm (6in) length of lilac ribbon and sew the ends securely to the outer edge of the remaining white felt circle.

6 Cover the back of the white felt snowflake with a thin drizzle of PVA (white) glue and carefully lay the snowflake onto the voile so that all three layers are sandwiched together.

5 Using a cocktail stick, drizzle a little PVA (white) glue along the outer edge of the plain white felt circle and carefully lay the voile circle on top, making sure that it has good contact with the adhesive.

Bells, Trees and Stars

Once you've made one Christmas-tree decoration, you'll want to make more, so templates are provided for other shapes – a bell, tree and star. These are made in basically the same way as the snowflake, with a slight modification for a couple of the designs, which is explained here.

Use the remaining felt, voile, seed bead and ribbons listed in the 'You will need' to make up the other decorations, referring to the photograph here and on page 27 as your guide and using the templates on page 116.

For the tree and star decorations with netting, use the templates to cut a tree shape and circle from blue netting. Once the voile layer has been glued in place, glue the netting over the voile layer in the same way before gluing the respective cutout shapes on top.

Denim and Daisy Elephant

This pretty, huggable elephant toy would be well loved by any new baby girl. Made in soft denim, it is embellished with fine decorative detail in the form of stylized flowers, quickly and cleverly applied using the technique of needle felting (see pages 10–12). The elephant's eyes, complete with endearing eyelashes, are worked in the same way, while the ears are simply edged in bold blanket stitch. To adapt the design for a boy, simply change the fleece colours to bright shades of blue and green, and create little star motifs instead of flowers.

The eye is needle felted, starting with the inner part of the eye in turquoise fleece, then the outer area worked in white fleece and finally the eyelashes in pink.

A small star stitch is embroidered in the centre of each needle-felted flower using six-stranded embroidery cotton (floss) in a contrasting tone.

Five-petalled flowers are needle felted to the denim on each side of the elephant.

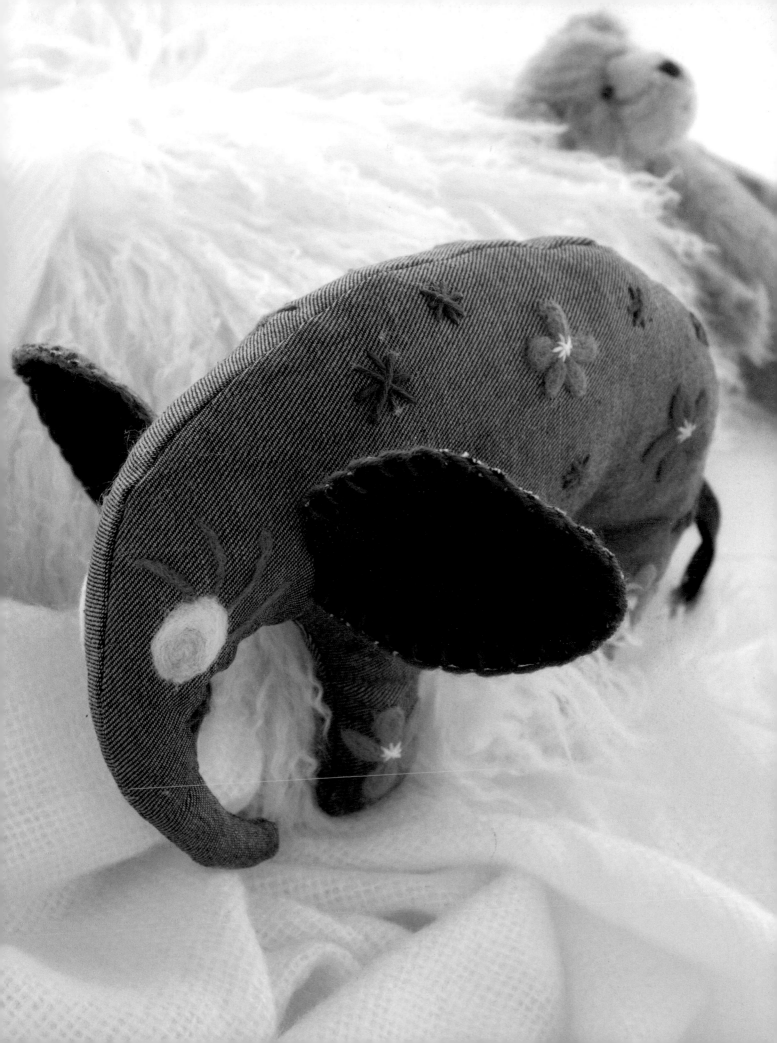

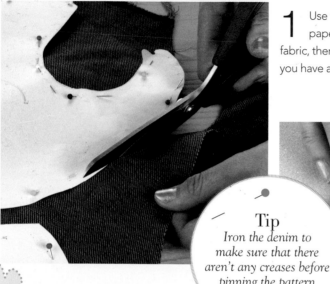

1 Use the templates on page 117 to cut an elephant body and an ear from paper. Use the paper pieces to cut one body and one ear from the denim fabric, then flip the patterns over and cut a second body and ear from denim so that you have a symmetrical pair of body pieces and a symmetrical pair of ears.

Tip
Iron the denim to make sure that there aren't any creases before pinning the pattern pieces onto it.

2 Using a chalk pencil, draw out a few flowers, either freehand or using the template on page 117. Place them at even intervals on each body piece. Lay the denim on the foam block. Using a medium-gauge felting needle with a small strand of pink fleece, begin to punch the needle through the fleece into the denim (see page 11). Follow the rough guide of the chalk marks until the whole of the flower has been needle felted. Work all the flowers in the same way.

3 Thread a needle with a length of embroidery cotton (floss) and carefully work a small star stitch (see page 21) through the centre of each flower, keeping them roughly the same size. Vary the colour of thread, using a lighter thread on a darker fleece colour and vice versa to achieve a good contrast.

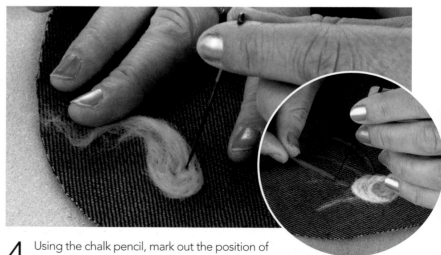

4 Using the chalk pencil, mark out the position of each eye. Loop a strand of turquoise fleece around your finger and place it in the marked-out area. Place the foam block under the fabric and needle felt the eye with a medium-gauge felting needle, stabbing through the fleece into the fabric until the whole area has been covered. Using a fine-gauge felting needle with the white fleece, work a crescent shape over the turquoise. Change to the pink fleece and work the eyelashes above the eye.

Tip
To ensure both ears are in the same position, draw through the slit with a chalk pencil and transfer the mark onto the other body piece.

5 Mark out a few stars in between the flowers with the chalk pencil. Thread a darning needle with a long length of fuchsia tapestry wool and work star stitches as before, keeping them all roughly the same size.

6 Using a sharp craft knife, make a slit for each ear just behind the eye, as indicated on the elephant body template. Fold each ear in half at the base to create some shape and secure with a few stitches. Using the tapestry wool, work blanket stitches (see page 21) around the ear. Repeat with the other ear. Place each ear in position on the elephant, pushing it through the slit, and pin on the wrong side. Machine stitch the ears in place.

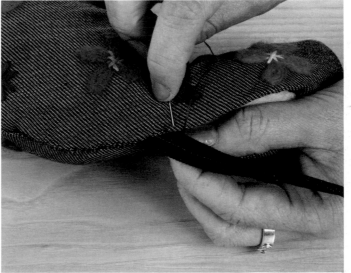

7 With right sides facing, pin the elephant body pieces together. Starting just above the tail height at the top of the back leg, carefully machine stitch around the elephant, using navy-blue sewing thread and taking a 6mm (¼in) seam allowance. Finish at the back ankle. Turn the elephant right side out through the gap. Stuff with the filling, using a blunt instrument, such as the end of a pencil, to compact the filling in the trunk and feet. Make sure that the elephant is well rounded.

8 Cut a strip of denim about 4 x 10cm (1½ x 4in), with one frayed short end. Fold in 1cm (⅜in) along the long edges and then fold into the centre to meet. Machine stitch close to either side of the centre. Place the tail, with the frayed end extending, into the gap in the body seam and sew securely in place with a few stitches. Pin the remaining gap closed. Using navy-blue thread, sew the opening together with 'invisible' slipstitches (see page 9).

Denim and Daisy Elephant 33

Favourite Jumper Bag

Nothing is worse than putting your favourite jumper into the washing machine only to take it out and find that it has shrunk to half its original size! But this tendency for woollens to shrink in the wash is put to good use here to create a wonderfully tactile bag. Don't use your favourite jumper, though. Instead, use an old woolly, perhaps one that no longer fits, or buy one from a charity or thrift store, looking out for knitwear with interesting patterns and features such as pocket details, ribbing and so on that you can incorporate into the design, as in the bag shown here.

The sides of the jumper/cardigan form the sides of the bag, so only the bottom edge needs to be stitched.

One of the sleeves is sewn to the top of the bag to create a decorative edging, while the other sleeve is cut in half to make the handles.

A fastening is made from a small green wet-felted ball and a loop cut from an offcut of the cardigan.

34

You will need

- Old woollen cardigan or jumper • Patterned lining fabric (see Step 7, page 38) • Synthetic felt, 25cm (10in) square – lime green and turquoise • 200g (7oz) of multipurpose polyester filling • 2 small wet-felted balls (see page 16) – green and turquoise • 14 turquoise beads, 5mm (¼in) in diameter • Green seed beads • Set square • Skewer • Sewing kit (see page 9)

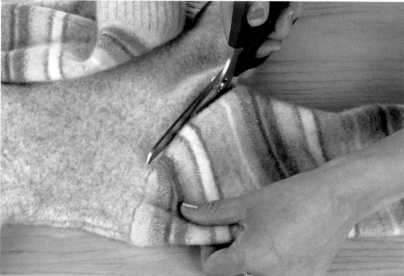

1 Wash your cardigan or jumper in the washing machine with an old pair of jeans to felt it (see page 7). Unpick the zip, if there is one, and discard it, then carefully hand stitch the opening together using neat little slipstitches. Cut off both the arms at the seams and put them to one side.

This is the cardigan from which the bag was made in its original form. You can utilize any interesting features or patterns that your chosen garment has to offer – in this case, the front opening, pockets, contrasting ribbing and striped sleeves.

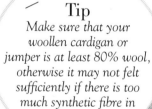

Tip
Make sure that your woollen cardigan or jumper is at least 80% wool, otherwise it may not felt sufficiently if there is too much synthetic fibre in the mix.

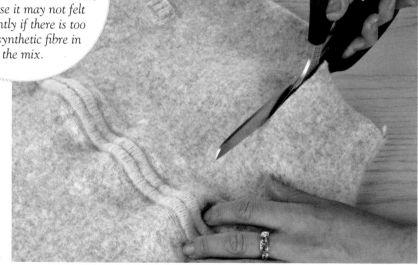

2 Using dressmaking scissors, cut right across the cardigan or jumper, just below the armholes. Discard the top section.

3 Turn the cardigan or jumper inside out and machine stitch along the bottom edge of the ribbing. The sides of the garment have now become the sides of the bag, so there is no need for any additional sewing.

Tip
Save the parts of the jumper that you don't need for the bag – you may be able to use them for other projects.

4 Cut one sleeve lengthwise in half and trim one half until it is 4cm (1½in) wide and long enough to wrap around the bag plus a small seam allowance. Join the ends to make a ring. Discard the other sleeve half. Pin the sleeve strip across the top of the inside of the bag and machine stitch in place. Turn the sleeve strip outwards over the top of the bag to create a collar. Curl the fabric under slightly and sew in place along the outside of the bag using neat little slipstitches.

5 Cut the remaining sleeve lengthways in half and trim each piece to 9 x 44cm (3½ x 17¼in). Pin the long sides of one sleeve piece together and machine stitch to form a handle. Pinch off small wads of polyester filling and use a skewer to stuff the handle until it is nicely rounded. Machine stitch the ends of the handle to close. Repeat with the other sleeve piece. Measure 5cm (2in) from each side of the bag and 3cm (1¼in) from the top of the bag and pin each end of the two handles in place. Hand stitch each handle in position, making sure that it is well secured.

6 Trim an offcut of the cardigan to 2 x 12cm (¾in x 4¾in) and fold it over to create a loop. Secure the loop with a couple of stitches and then hand stitch it centrally onto the back top edge of the bag. On the front of the bag in a corresponding position, sew on a green wet-felted ball to create a fastener.

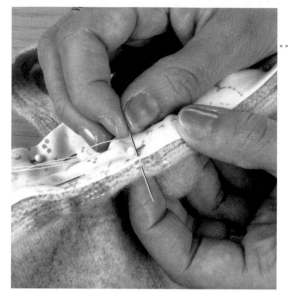

7 With right sides facing, fold the lining fabric in half. Measure the width and height of the bag. Using a set square, measure and draw out a rectangle the same size on the lining fabric, with the fold along the bottom edge. Cut out the rectangle, cutting through both layers of fabric. Machine stitch the sides together, taking a 6mm (¼in) seam allowance. Turn over and press down a 2cm (¾in) seam around the top edge. Push the lining into the bag and pin it to the inside of the bag just below the top edge. Stitch in place using 'invisible' slipstitches (see page 9).

8 Using the template on page 118, cut out the flower centre and petal from paper. Pin the flower centre template to the lime green felt and cut out. Using the petal template, cut out five petals from turquoise felt.

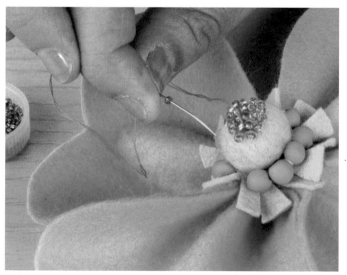

9 Snip around the outer edge of the flower centre with embroidery scissors. Pinch each of the petals at the base to create a 3-D shape and secure with a few stitches.

10 Assemble the corsage by sewing all the petals together at the base, then sewing the flower centre in position. Sew the turquoise wet-felted ball in the centre of the flower, then sew the turquoise beads around the ball. Sew a cluster of green seeds beads to the top of the ball. Carefully stitch the corsage in place in the top right-hand corner of the bag.

Fair Isle Bag

The shape, style and pattern of the jumper you choose will to some extent dictate the design of your finished bag. In this variation, the jumper was plain in style, but its Fair Isle pattern and colours were striking and have actually been accentuated by the felting process to produce a highly attractive felt fabric.

To add interest to the basic shape of this bag, trim off the sleeves and neck and then cut the remaining fabric into two rectangles with inward sloping sides for the bag front and back. Stitch the bottom and sides of the rectangles with right sides facing. The leather handles shown here were salvaged from an old bag, but you could use the sleeve fabric for handles, as explained in Step 5, page 37, or buy or salvage some. Stitch a row of large coordinating buttons to the front of the bag for some contemporary-style detailing.

Paisley Purse

The wet-felting technique has been used here to make the base fabric for this dainty bag, which involves laying down fibres of fleece, then applying water, soap and friction to bond them (see pages 14–16). Because the bag is cleverly designed from one long strip of felt fabric simply folded over and requiring only two seams, it is quick and easy to make up. Paisley motifs have been worked into the homemade felt fabric using the needle-felting technique (see pages 10–12), with seed beads and embroidered flowers added to give a textural and three-dimensional quality to the pattern.

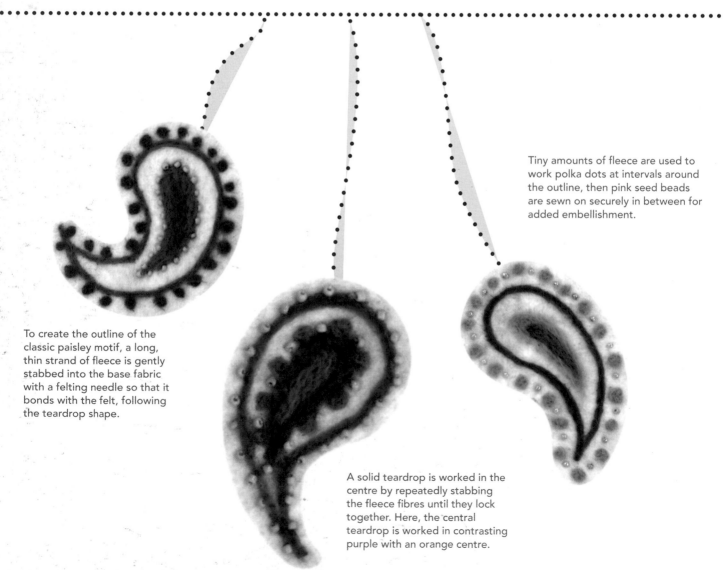

Tiny amounts of fleece are used to work polka dots at intervals around the outline, then pink seed beads are sewn on securely in between for added embellishment.

To create the outline of the classic paisley motif, a long, thin strand of fleece is gently stabbed into the base fabric with a felting needle so that it bonds with the felt, following the teardrop shape.

A solid teardrop is worked in the centre by repeatedly stabbing the fleece fibres until they lock together. Here, the central teardrop is worked in contrasting purple with an orange centre.

You will need

- Homemade white felt fabric 70 x 35cm (27½ x 13¾in) (see pages 14–16) • Small quantities of carded fleece – purple and orange in two different shades plus green and pink • Seed beads – pink and green • 1 skein of pale green six-stranded embroidery cotton (floss) • 1 pair of Velcro spots (hook and loop fastening) • 1 decorative button • Needle-felting equipment (see page 10) • Sewing kit (see page 9)

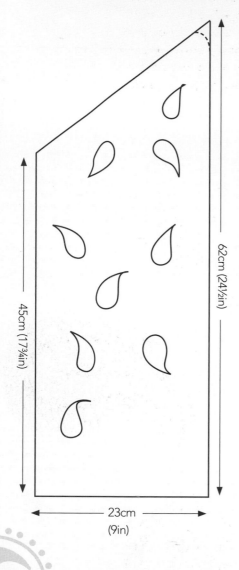

62cm (24½in)

45cm (17¾in)

23cm (9in)

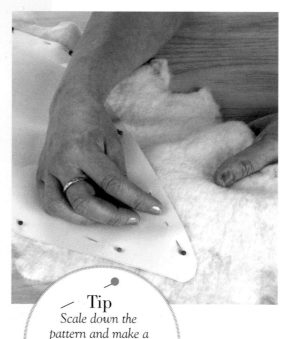

1 Referring to the diagram (left), on a piece of scrap paper, draw out a rectangle 62 x 23cm (24½ x 9in). Mark a point 45cm (17¾in) up one long side. Draw a line from the top of the opposite long side to join the mark to form a sharp angle at the top of the rectangle. Cut out the template. Carefully pin the template to the felt and cut around it, keeping as close to the paper edge as possible. Remove the template and round off the point, as indicated on the diagram.

Tip
Scale down the pattern and make a miniature version for a matching coin purse, omitting the handle.

2 Lay your felt over the foam block. Using a chalk pencil, draw out the teardrop shapes in varying sizes at evenly spaced intervals over the felt, either freehand or using the templates on page 118. Gently pull off a long piece of purple fleece about 6mm (¼in) wide. Starting at the tip of one teardrop shape and using a medium-gauge felting needle, gently stab the fleece into the felt to bond the layers together (see page 12). Continue in the same way to form the teardrop shape.

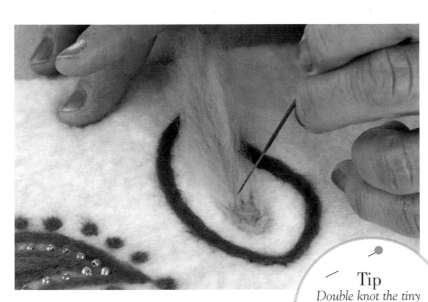

3 Change to the green fleece and work a smaller teardrop shape in the centre of the larger shape, repeatedly stabbing the fibres until they lock together. Using a small amount of the purple fleece, work another teardrop shape in the centre of the green fleece, following the shape of the motif (see page 12).

Tip
Double knot the tiny beads before and after you sew on each one; that way, if you lose one, you won't lose them all.

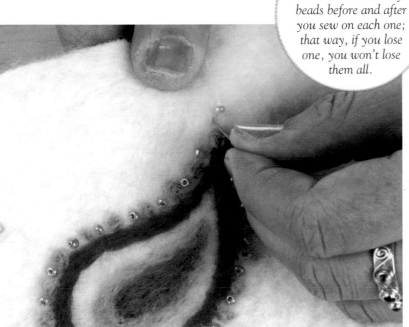

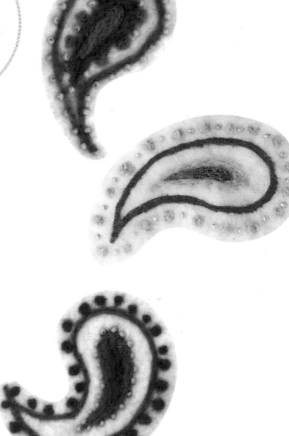

4 Using small amounts of the green fleece, work little polka dots (see page 12) around the outside of the complete paisley motif, keeping them as close to the edge as possible. Thread a needle with a double length of white sewing thread. Start at the tip of the paisley motif and sew a pink seed bead in between each of the green polka dots. Sew each one on twice to ensure that they are well secured and finish with a knot on the back of the fabric.

5 Work the remaining paisley motifs in the same way, varying the fleece colours used from shape to shape and changing the colour and position of the beads.

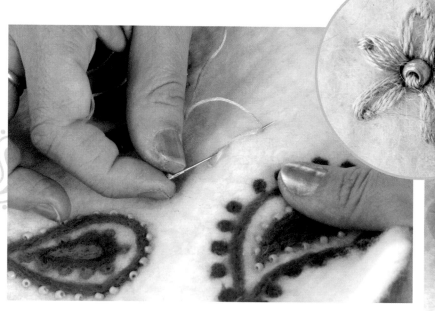

6 Using pale green embroidery cotton (floss), randomly embroider lazy-daisy stitches (see page 21) between the paisley motifs. Secure the ends with a knot. Sew a pink seed bead in the centre of each flower, passing the thread through the bead twice for added security.

Tip
To create really neat lazy-daisy stitches, mark the centre of each flower and the points of four or five petals before you stitch.

7 Lay the felt rectangle vertically, pointed end upwards, and with the motif side downwards. Fold the bottom third up to cover the central third and pin in place. Machine stitch up one side and then the other, taking a 6mm (¼in) seam allowance. Using slipstitch, hand stitch one part of the Velcro spot (hook and loop fastening) on the underside of the flap. Fold the flap over the bag front, make a corresponding mark on the bag front and sew on the remaining part.

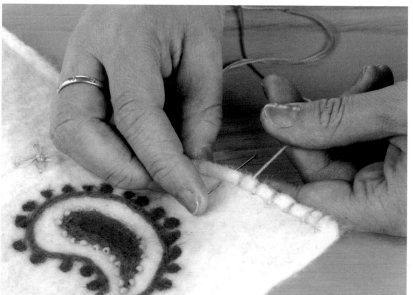

8 Thread a needle with a long length of green embroidery cotton (floss) and work blanket stitches (see page 21) down the sides of the bag, across the top of the bag and around the sides of the flap.

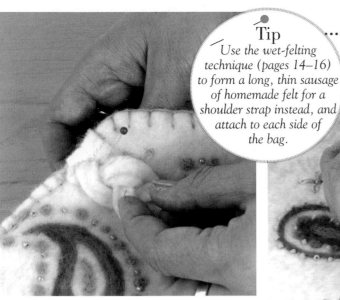

Tip
Use the wet-felting technique (pages 14–16) to form a long, thin sausage of homemade felt for a shoulder strap instead, and attach to each side of the bag.

9 From the remaining felt, cut three strips 1 x 23cm (⅜ x 9in). Using white thread, hand stitch the ends of all three strips together, then loosely plait (braid) the strips. Secure the other ends together with a few stitches. Pin one end of the plait (braid) 6cm (2⅜in) from each side of the bag at the top and machine stitch in place.

10 Sew the button on the front of the bag, roughly corresponding to where the fastening is positioned.

Beaded Bag Charm

This stylish charm made from store-bought felt will add the perfect finishing touch to any bag, although it would look equally effective adorning a purse or a key ring. Coordinate the colour scheme with your favourite bag or outfit, or make mini versions for your mobile (cell) phone.

Cut out two lilac felt circles about 5cm (2in) in diameter. Use pinking shears to cut out a green felt circle about 4cm (1½in) in diameter and a pink felt circle slightly smaller than the green circle. Fold a length of pink ribbon over to form a loop and sew to one side of a lilac felt circle. Thread a few different-sized silver balls onto three lengths of green embroidery cotton (floss), each knotted at one end, and sew in place opposite the ribbon. Using the green embroidery cotton (floss), embroider a lazy-daisy stitch (see page 21) in the centre of the pink felt circle and decorate with a few pink seed beads. Assemble the charm by gluing the second lilac circle behind the first, sandwiching the ribbon loop and beaded threads in between. Now glue the remaining felt circles on top of each other on the front. Finish by working blanket stitch (see page 21) around the outer edge in green.

Beautiful Bird Mobile

This hypnotic mobile would look enchanting swaying in the nursery or fluttering around on a landing near an open window. The exotic birds are reminiscent of birds of paradise and the bright colours will provide an ideal first focus of attention for a very young baby. The birds are ingeniously modelled around a rolled-up core of fleece using the needle-felting technique (see pages 10–13), which is also employed to add colour variations and detailing to the bird forms. Wet-felted balls (see page 16) suspended on colourful ribbons from a simple wood plinth add further interest.

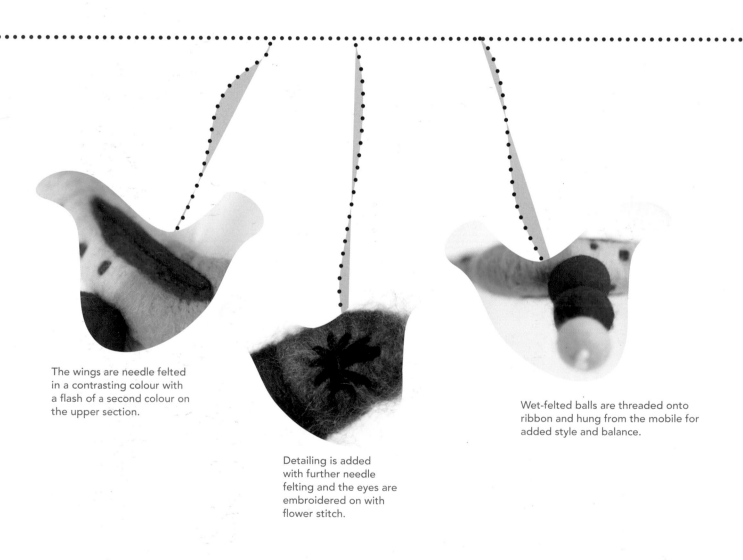

The wings are needle felted in a contrasting colour with a flash of a second colour on the upper section.

Detailing is added with further needle felting and the eyes are embroidered on with flower stitch.

Wet-felted balls are threaded onto ribbon and hung from the mobile for added style and balance.

You will need

• 30g (1oz) of carded fleece – turquoise, aqua, red, pink, plum and purple • Small amounts of carded fleece – dark blue and orange • 1 skein of black six-stranded embroidery cotton (floss) • 0.5m (½yd) each of narrow ribbon – aqua, lilac, red, pink, blue and purple • About 22 wet-felted balls (see page 16), varying in size and in coordinating colours • 5mm (¼in) thick MDF, about 30cm (12in) square • Compass • Workbench • Safety goggles and dust mask • Jigsaw • Drill with 3mm (⅛in) drill bit • Fine sandpaper • Test pot of white emulsion paint • Decorator's paintbrush • Needle-felting equipment (see page 10) • Large darning needle • Sewing kit (see page 9)

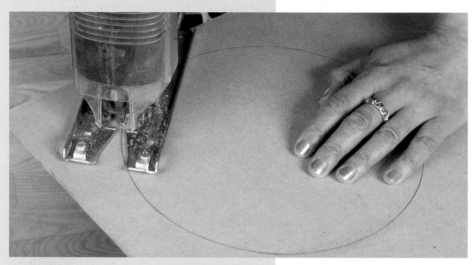

1 Using a compass, draw a 21cm (8¼in) diameter circle on the piece of MDF. Place the wood on a workbench. Wearing safety goggles and a dust mask, carefully cut out the circle with a jigsaw.

Tip
If you are not confident using power tools, ask your wood supplier to cut the circle from the MDF for you.

2 Mark six points on the wood circle 2cm (¾in) from the outer edge and 9cm (3½in) apart, and one point in the centre. Using the drill, accurately drill a hole through each of the pencil marks. Rub down any rough edges with fine sandpaper.

3 Give the back and front of the MDF circle two coats of the white emulsion paint, waiting for the first coat to dry before applying the second.

4 Work over a large foam block, keeping your fingers well out of the way of the needles. Pull off a long strip of turquoise fleece and roll it up to form the core of the bird. Pull off another long strip and wind it around the core, then begin to stab the fleece repeatedly with a medium-gauge multi-needle felting tool until the fleece no longer comes away when you pull it and it becomes denser and thicker.

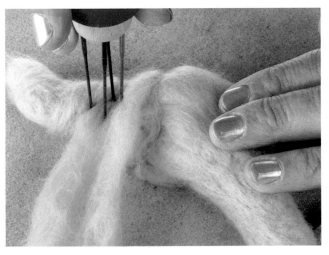

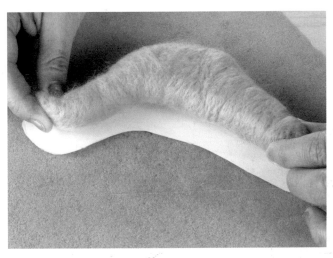

5 Continue to give shape to the bird by forming the tail with your hands and needle felting more fleece to form the head and body. Add bulk to the bird by wrapping thin strips of fleece around the shape by hand and creating a denser form with the multi-needle felting tool.

6 Check the shape of your bird against the template on page 119 to make sure that its basic form is progressing in the right way.

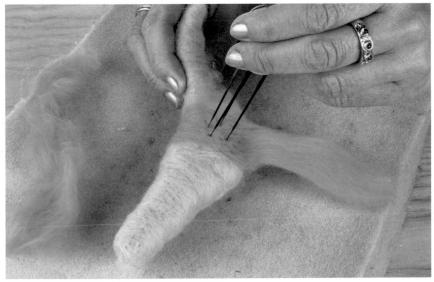

7 Pull off a strip of aqua fleece measuring about 6cm (2½in) wide and wrap it around the breast area of the bird, stabbing it repeatedly with the multi-needle felting tool until it becomes a part of the base fabric. Wrap a smaller strip around the beak and use a fine-gauge felting needle to needle felt it to the bird.

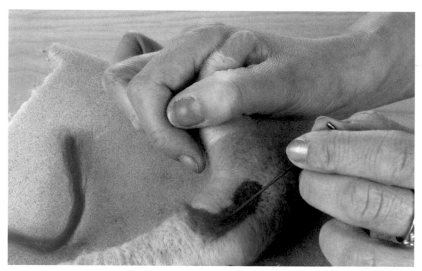

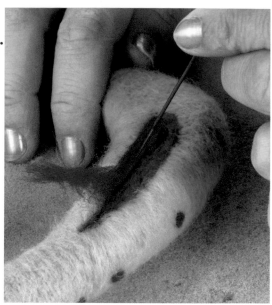

8 Pull off small wisps of dark blue fleece and randomly needle felt about seven 'speckles' on the underside of the bird with the felting needle. Refer to the template on page 119 as your guide. Lay a length of dark blue fleece across the centre of the body where the wing should be and needle felt it onto the body in a large teardrop shape. Work the other side of the body in the same way, keeping both sides symmetrical.

9 Continue to build up the wing pattern, needle felting a flash of red through the wing. Work the other side in the same way.

Tip

If you need lots of fairly small amounts of felt colours, as here, ask your supplier if they can provide a mixed or sample pack.

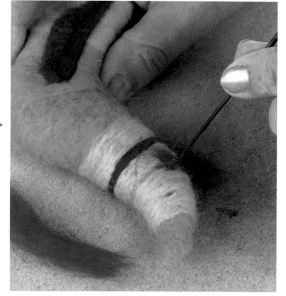

10 Pull off a fine, even strand of red fleece and wrap it around the neck of the bird. Using the felting needle, repeatedly stab the strand, working all the way around the neck as you do so. Work another ring in the same way.

11 Thread a needle with a length of black embroidery cotton (floss) and work a flower stitch in the centre of the head (see page 21), pushing the needle through the head to work the other side in the same way.

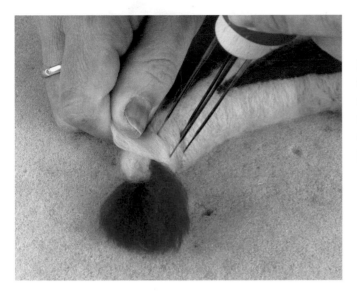

12 Pull off a tuft of dark blue fleece 3.5cm (1½in) long. Position on top of the bird's body, near the tail, and hold it in place with your finger. Wrap a strip of turquoise fleece around the tuft to stop it from moving and stab repeatedly until it becomes a part of the bird's body. Work two other birds in the same way, referring to the template on page 119 for the form, pattern and detailing, but varying the fleece colours used, as shown in the main photograph on page 47.

13 Tie a knot at the end of a length of aqua ribbon. Using a large darning needle, thread on two or three wet-felted balls in coordinating colours. Push the needle through the underside of the bird until it comes out through the top of its back. Measure 30cm (12in) up from the bird's back and tie the ribbon in a knot, then thread on two or three more balls. Repeat with the other birds, varying the colours and lengths of the ribbon.

Tip

As well as serving an aesthetic purpose, the wet-felted balls act to balance the mobile. Add balls or take them away until you are happy with the overall appearance and balance of the mobile.

14 Fold over a 10cm (4in) length of ribbon to form a loop. Using the darning needle, thread both ends through a small wet-felted ball, then pull both ends through the hole in the centre of the wood and knot on the underside. Using the darning needle, thread each bird's ribbon through a hole around the outside of the plinth and thread on a coordinating wet-felted ball. Knot the ends of the ribbons and trim the excess to finish.

Rustic Beret

This stylish beret is perfect for keeping out those chilly winter winds. This example is worked in rich autumnal shades of rust and brown, but gold and red tones or even greens and yellows would look equally stunning. The beret is constructed from just two pieces of felt fabric, one for the crown and the other for the brim, then simply machine stitched together. Individual oak leaves have been cut out and sewn onto the brim using either backstitch or decorative French knots (see pages 20–21), with little pink and gold beads adding to the embellishment.

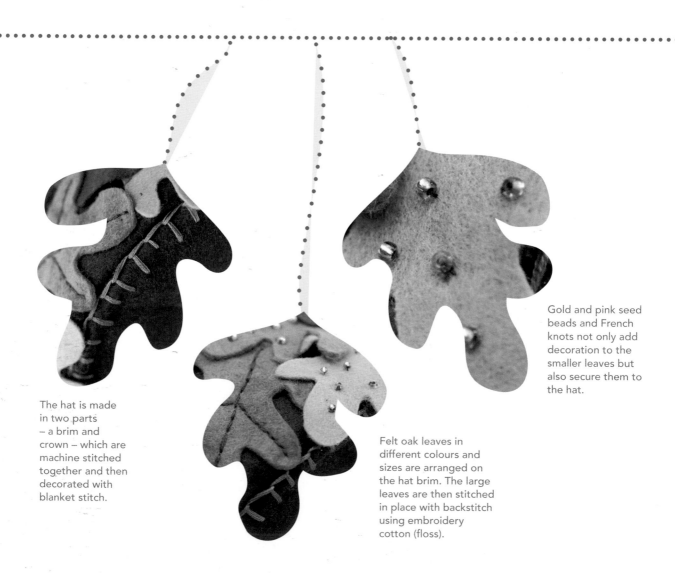

Gold and pink seed beads and French knots not only add decoration to the smaller leaves but also secure them to the hat.

The hat is made in two parts – a brim and crown – which are machine stitched together and then decorated with blanket stitch.

Felt oak leaves in different colours and sizes are arranged on the hat brim. The large leaves are then stitched in place with backstitch using embroidery cotton (floss).

You will need

- 1m (1yd) of dark brown synthetic felt • Synthetic felt, 25cm (10in) square – beige, ginger, buff, rust and mid brown • 1 skein each of six-stranded embroidery cotton (floss) – rust, red and brown • Seed beads – gold, pink and bronze • Masking tape • Compass • Sewing kit (see page 9

1 Measure the circumference of the head of the person for whom the beret is intended at its widest point. Transfer the measurement onto a 10cm (4in) wide strip of stiff paper, then join the ends of the paper together with a piece of masking tape to create a ring. Measure the radius of the ring. Using a compass, draw a circle the same size on another piece of stiff paper and then carefully cut out.

Tip

For a slightly different look, instead of using synthetic felt, the same pattern can be made using knitwear that has been felted in the washing machine (see page 7).

2 Pin the paper circle – the template for the crown – onto the dark brown felt and carefully cut around it. Remove the masking tape from the paper ring. Pin the strip – the template for the brim – to the dark brown felt and carefully cut out, as shown.

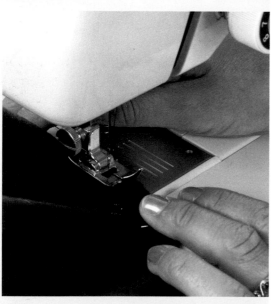

3 Pin the ends of the brim together and machine stitch, taking a 6mm (¼in) seam allowance. Pin the brim to the crown, making sure that the stitched seam of the brim is on the outside. Carefully machine stitch the two pieces together. Take your time when sewing to ensure that you achieve a good shape to your finished hat. Turn the beret right side out.

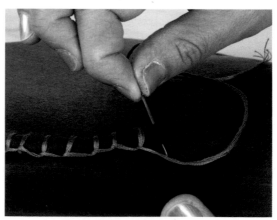

4 Thread a needle with three strands of rust embroidery cotton (floss) and start working neat blanket stitches around the seam (see page 21), where the brim joins the crown. Continue working all the way around the beret.

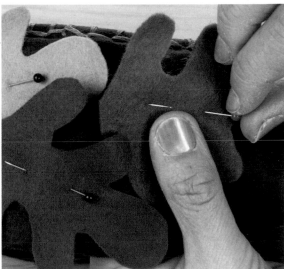

6 Lay the oak leaves all around the hat, overlapping them and interspersing the small leaves between the larger ones for variety. Once you are happy with their final position, pin them in place.

5 Using the templates on page 119, cut out the small and large oak leaves from paper. Pin the small leaf template to the felt and use embroidery scissors to cut out about eight small leaves in a variety of brown shades. Cut out about 12 large oak leaves in different browns in the same way.

Tip
You don't have to use oak leaves. Maple leaves have lovely shapes too, or you could use several different leaf shapes for your beret design.

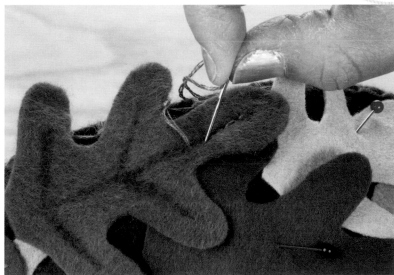

7 Using a fade-away marker, draw a central vein and side veins onto the large oak leaves. Use three strands of embroidery cotton (floss) to stitch the veins in backstitch (see page 20), stitching through the brim of the fabric to secure the leaves to the beret and alternating between using the rust and red thread from leaf to leaf.

8 Thread a needle with a double length of ordinary brown thread and randomly sew gold and pink seed beads onto half the small leaves, stitching through the rim fabric to secure the leaves to the beret. Embellish the brim with a row of bronze seed beads. Using three strands of embroidery cotton (floss), work about six French knots in rust, red and brown over each of the remaining small oak leaves (see page 21).

Springtime Egg Hangings

Spring is the time of re-birth and renewal, and the egg is its enduring symbol, with many cultures having a tradition of decorating eggs in their different ways. These egg hangings have a wonderful textural appeal as well as lovely colour interest. They are quickly created by needle felting coloured fleece onto egg-shaped polystyrene formers (see page 13), and cleverly embellished with pretty needle-felted patterns (see page 12) and flower sequins that can be glued or pinned in place. Other embellishments can also be added – use whatever you have in your craft box that looks good.

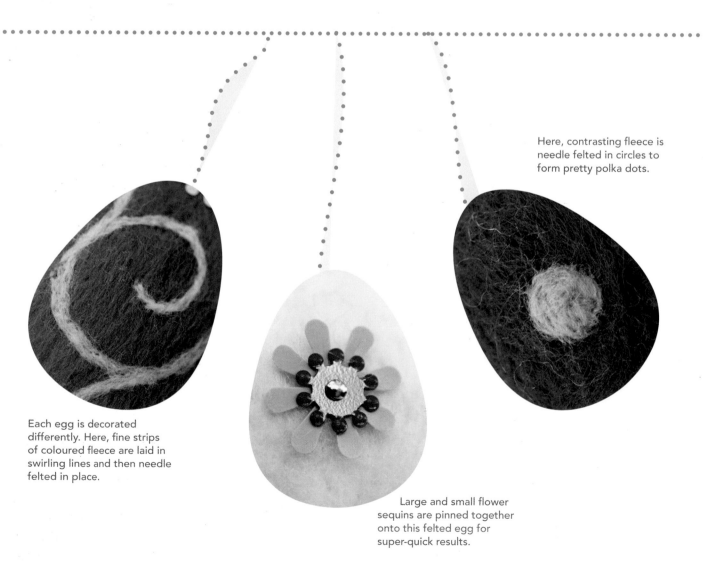

Here, contrasting fleece is needle felted in circles to form pretty polka dots.

Each egg is decorated differently. Here, fine strips of coloured fleece are laid in swirling lines and then needle felted in place.

Large and small flower sequins are pinned together onto this felted egg for super-quick results.

You will need

• 30g (1oz) of carded fleece – lilac, yellow, lime green, green, purple and pink • 0.5m (½yd) of narrow ribbon – yellow, pink, pale pink, rose pink and green • Large flower sequins – 20 yellow and 12 lilac • Small flower sequins – 12 red and 12 pale pink • 3 large egg-shaped polystyrene formers • 4 small egg-shaped polystyrene formers • Needle-felting equipment (see page 10) • PVA (white) glue • Sewing kit (see page 9)

1 Pull off a long strip of the lilac fleece and wrap it around one of the large polystyrene eggs.

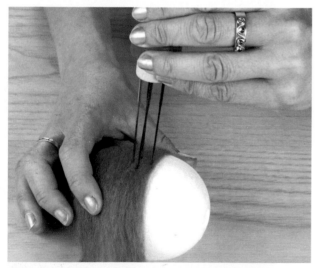

2 Using a medium-gauge multi-needle felting tool, repeatedly stab the fleece into the polystyrene so that it no longer comes away when you gently pull it. Turn the egg around and continue stabbing until a section of the egg has been covered. Pull off another strip of fleece and continue working around the egg until it is completely covered and the felt has thickened. Any thin areas can be filled in by needle felting wisps of the fleece.

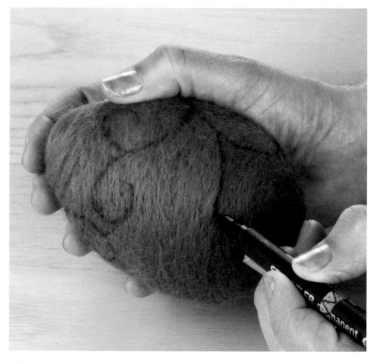

3 Using egg template A on page 120 as a guide, draw a spiral pattern onto the fleece-covered egg with a fine marker pen. The pattern doesn't have to be precise – any quirkiness is part of the charm.

4 Pull off a thin strip of yellow fleece and lay it over the lines of the design. Using a medium-gauge felting needle, stab the fleece into the egg, following the lines as you do so, remembering to keep your fingers out of the way of the needle at all times (see page 12). Work small areas at a time until the whole pattern has been completed.

Tip
For added sparkle, attach a small rhinestone or flat-backed jewel to the centre of each flower sequin.

5 Using a cocktail stick, apply evenly spaced dots of PVA (white) glue between the gaps in the design, then stick down the yellow flower sequins.

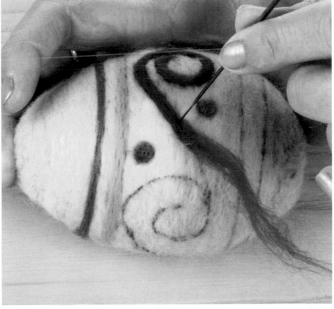

6 Again using a cocktail stick, make a hole in the top of the egg by pushing the stick through the fleece and into the polystyrene. Cut a 10cm (4in) length of yellow ribbon, form it into a loop and tie the ends together in a knot. Push the knotted ends into the hole and secure them with a dot of glue.

7 Using the multi-needle felting tool, needle felt another large egg with lime green fleece, as in Steps 1 and 2. Using the egg template B on page 120 as a guide, draw the band of spirals and dots and the parallel lines above and below onto the fleece-covered egg with the marker pen. Using a fine-gauge felting needle, needle felt the pattern, including the polka dots (see page 12), changing the fleece colours as required. Fold over a length of pink ribbon and attach it to the top, as in Step 6.

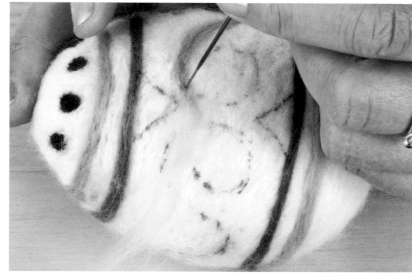

8 Using the multi-needle felting tool, needle felt the remaining large polystyrene egg with yellow fleece, as in Steps 1 and 2 on page 58. Using the egg template C on page 120 as a guide, draw the pattern onto the fleece-covered egg with the marker pen, needle felt the pattern using the fine-gauge felting needle and attach a ribbon loop to the top, as in Step 6 on page 59.

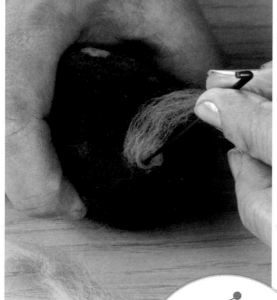

9 Using the multi-needle felting tool, needle felt a small polystyrene egg with purple fleece, as in Steps 1 and 2 on page 58. Pull off a small strip of green fleece and needle felt a small polka dot, as in Step 7 on page 59. Continue working polka dots randomly over the whole surface of the egg in different colours. Attach a loop of green ribbon, as in Step 6 on page 59. Repeat with a second small polystyrene egg but needle felting it in pink fleece and attaching a pale pink ribbon loop.

Tip
Display the eggs hung onto long stems of willow or grouped together in a large glass bowl for an eye-catching centrepiece.

10 For super-quick decoration, felt your egg in yellow as explained in Steps 1 and 2 on page 58, then use a pin to attach each small red flower sequin to the centre of a large lilac one. Push the pins into the egg to complete the decorations, spacing them evenly. Make a pink ribbon hanging loop as explained in Step 6 on page 59. Decorate the remaining eggs in the same ways.

Felted Christmas Baubles

These colourful Christmas tree decorations are created in exactly the same way as the egg hangings, but using round polystyrene formers in various different sizes ranging from 4cm (1½in) to 26cm (10in).

Use traditional colours for the fleece to cover the balls including red and green, plus a few more unusual colours such as turquoise, aqua, yellow and lime green for added excitement. Cover the balls as in Steps 1 and 2 on page 58. The templates for the three different needle-felting patterns are given on page 121, and should be worked in contrasting colours onto the fleece-covered balls in the same way as for the eggs. For quick and easy variations, balls can be decorated with pinned-on flower sequins (see Step 10 opposite) or beads – try using a variety of sizes and colours. You can also vary the fleece colours – it can look very stylish to limit yourself to just two contrasting colours for all the tree decorations.

Vibrant Document Bag

This distinctively designed bag is a great way of transporting your documents safely. Slightly larger than A4/US letter size, it is ideal for carrying magazines and books alike. The bag is very easily constructed from a folded rectangular piece of sturdy felt fabric, with the side seams stitched on the outside for a rustic finish. The cutout design for the bag front is simply glued to vibrant orange hand-carded Nepal felted wool (see page 6) to make a bold impact with the minimum of effort. The bag is fastened with a false felt button, which conceals a popper fastener underneath the flap.

The rabbit and flower design is cut in the end of a large rectangle of cerise felt to form the front flap and then glued to a piece of contrasting orange felt.

A handle made from a strip of leftover felt is machine stitched to the bag back around the edges and diagonally for extra strength.

A wet-felted ball is sewn centrally to the bottom edge of the front flap in the position of a hidden popper fastener.

You will need

- Cerise dyed wool felt fabric (see page 7), 120 x 46cm (48 x 18in) • Orange Nepal wool felt fabric (see page 6), 30 x 42cm (12 x 16½in) • 1 small pink wet-felted ball (see page 16) • Pink seed beads • 1 pair of popper fasteners • Fabric glue and plastic spreader • Sewing kit (see page 9)

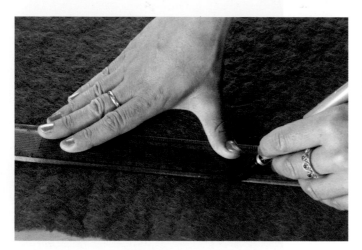

1 Using a long ruler and a fade-away marker, draw a rectangle onto the cerise felt fabric measuring 86.5 x 35cm (34 x 13¾in).

Tip

If your wool fabric is not long enough to cut the rectangle out in a single piece, cut a piece two-thirds the length, then join on the extra one-third for the flap, allowing for a 6mm (¼in) seam, so that the join runs along the top of the flap and is less obvious.

2 Using the template on page 121 and embroidery scissors, cut out the design from paper. Pin the template to the felt fabric so that it aligns with the bottom edge and sides of the rectangle. Carefully cut out the inner areas of the pattern – take your time, as inaccurate cutting will show up in your finished work. Then cut out around the bottom and sides of the template and around the remainder of the rectangle. Remove the template.

3 Using the marker, measure and mark out a 4cm (1½in) wide strip 28cm (11in) long from the remaining cerise felt fabric for a handle. Cut out the strip.

4 Measure and mark 33cm (13in) from the bottom edge of the rectangle and 11cm (4¼in) from each side. Pin one end of the handle to the bag at each mark, with the loop of the handle facing towards the cutout design/bottom edge of the rectangle, and machine stitch around each handle end, then diagonally from corner to corner, to strengthen the handle.

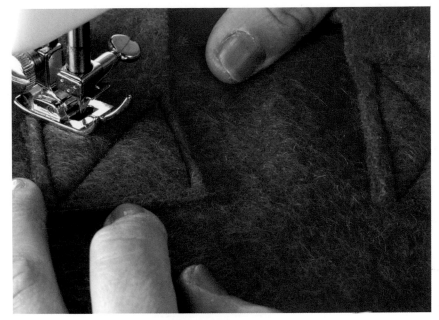

5 Pour a little of the fabric glue into a tray, and using a plastic spreader, spread the glue over the reverse of the cutout design, being careful not to apply too much and taking it right to the sides of the cut edges. Once the design has been covered, lay the orange felt over the design and gently press down with your fingers so that both pieces make good contact. Leave for at least ten minutes for the glue to go off slightly before trimming the orange felt to size, using the cerise felt fabric as a guide.

6 Turn the cerise felt fabric over and the other way around so that the felt-backed design is now at the top of the rectangle. Pin a 1cm (⅜in) hem along the bottom edge of the rectangle, which will form the edge of the bag opening when the rectangle is folded up. Hand stitch in place with neat slipstitches.

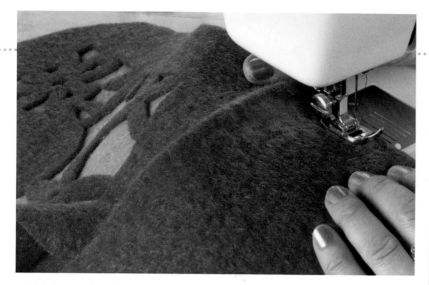

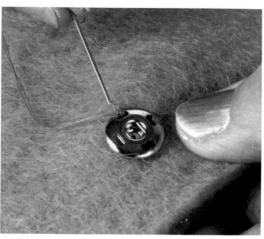

7 Fold the bottom third of the rectangle of felt up over the central third. Pin both sides together and machine stitch in place, taking in a 6mm (¼in) seam allowance.

8 On the reverse of what will be the front flap of the bag, measure and mark 2.5cm (1in) from the bottom edge of the flap at the midway point across the width of the flap. Sew the base of the popper fastener at the mark. Fold the flap down over the bag front and mark the corresponding position of the other part of the popper fastener on the bag front. Sew securely in place.

9 Hand stitch about six pink seed beads onto the pink wet-felted ball, securing each bead with a knot before moving on to the next one.

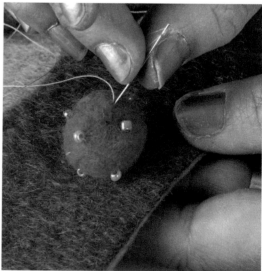

Tip
Choose other colours of felt for the bag, but make sure they are contrasting so that the pattern stands out from the background. Using the combination of a pale and a dark colour would also give an effective result.

10 Thread a needle with a double length of pink thread and sew the wet-felted ball on the front flap of the bag, over the popper fastener on the reverse of the flap and front of the bag.

11 Sew pink seed beads all the way around the outer edge of the front flap, spaced about 3cm (1¼in) apart, knotting the thread before and after each bead has been added.

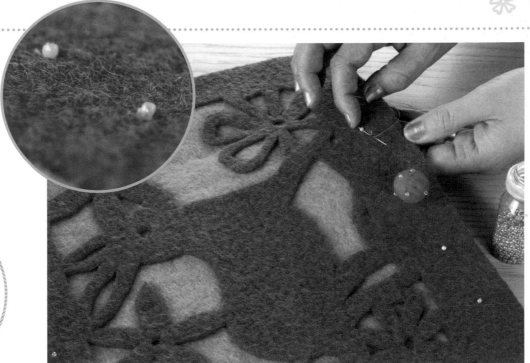

Tip
Once the bag is finished, iron the design – the heat helps to bond the glue to the fabric, making the bag stronger overall.

These rabbit and flower motifs are reminiscent of Bavarian paper cuts, which are traditionally quite complicated designs cut out of a single sheet of paper. Here, this technique has been cleverly transferred to felt fabric in a simplified form, for visual impact and speed.

Collar Necklace

Pamper yourself with this exquisite three-stranded collar necklace, ingeniously created using small wet-felted balls as beads (see page 16), and embellished with sparkling sequins and seed beads. The felt beads are cleverly fixed in place with crimp beads so that they remain suspended on their gossamer-like strands of wire. Real silver beads nestle either side of the felt beads for a touch of opulence. Team up the bead colour with a favourite outfit or coordinate the necklace with accessories, such as a bag or shoes. And why not make a few extra balls to string up a matching bracelet?

Wet-felted balls in three sizes are embellished with bead-topped sequins.

Sets of balls, with a silver bead either side, are threaded onto lengths of wire and secured at evenly spaced intervals with crimp beads.

The strands are attached to a separator and then to a simple clasp.

You will need

- Green wet-felted felt balls (see page 16) – 6 x 3cm (1¼in), 5 x 2.5cm (1in) and 4 x 2cm (¾in) in diameter
- About 100 green sequins • About 100 small green glass beads • About 40 silver crimp beads/tubes
- Sterling silver beads – 12 x 6mm (¼in), 10 x 4mm (⅛in) and 14 x 2mm (³/₃₂in) in diameter • 1.5m (60in) length of tiger tail • 2 sterling silver three-ring separators • 2 sterling silver jump rings, 6mm (¼in) in diameter
- 1 sterling silver S-hook and chain clasp • Large darning needle • White chinagraph pencil • Pair of pliers
- Sewing kit (see page 9)

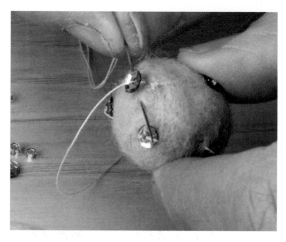

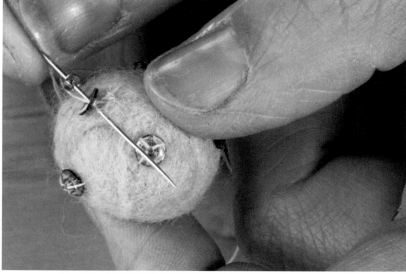

1 Thread a needle with a length of green thread and sew the sequins onto the wet-felted balls, spacing them about 2cm (¾in) apart. Push the needle right through to the other side of the ball in order to work the next sequin. Work all the balls in the same way, securing the thread after working the last sequin.

2 Thread a needle with green thread and sew a green bead into the centre of each of the sequins, pushing the needle back through the bead so that it comes out through the sequin on the opposite side of the ball. Continue until all 15 wet-felted balls have been embellished in the same way. Knot securely after the final bead.

Tip
Look out for crimping pliers from jewellery-making suppliers, which make crimping really neat and easy.

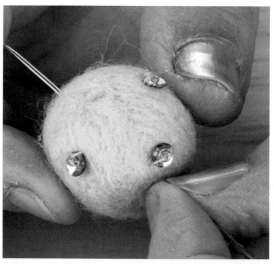

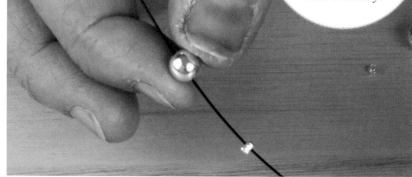

3 Using a large darning needle, make a pilot hole in each ball by pushing the needle right through the centre. This will make threading them onto the wire much easier.

4 For the outer (longest) strand, cut a 50cm (20in) length of tiger tail. Using a white chinagraph pencil, mark 8cm (3in) from the end of the wire. Slide a crimp bead up the wire to the mark. Use pliers to squeeze the crimp closed. Now thread a 6mm (¼in) silver bead onto the wire, butting it up against the crimp.

5 Using the pilot hole, thread one of the 3cm (1¼in) wet-felted balls onto the wire, then thread on another 6mm (¼in) silver bead and squeeze on a crimp bead, as in Step 4. Continue threading the remaining 3cm (1¼in) balls, 6mm (¼in) silver beads and crimp beads onto the wire, leaving a gap of 2.5cm (1in) between the sets of beads.

6 For the middle strand, cut a 44cm (17¼in) length of tiger tail. Secure the first crimp bead 10cm (4in) from the end, then thread on 4mm (⅛in) silver beads and 2.5cm (1in) wet-felted balls, as before, leaving a gap of 2cm (¾in) between sets. For the inner strand, cut a 37cm (14½in) length of tiger tail. Secure the first crimp bead 12cm (4¾in) from the end, then thread on 2mm (³⁄₃₂in) silver beads and 2cm (¾in) wet-felted balls as before, leaving a gap of 1cm (⅜in) between sets. Lay all three strands in order, positioning them so that the felt balls of each strand sit in between the ones above them. Trim the ends of the wires, if necessary, to adjust the length.

Tip
Use the best jewellery findings money can buy – sterling silver (or 9-carat gold if changing the colour scheme) are always worth investing in and will make a great difference to the overall look and feel of your jewellery.

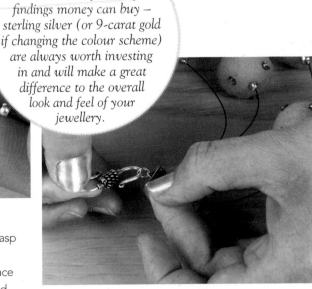

7 Using pliers, open one of the jump rings and thread it onto the single ring of one of the separators (not shown). Thread the end link of the clasp chain onto the jump ring, then close it with the pliers. Now thread a crimp bead and then a 2mm (³⁄₃₂in) silver bead onto the end of the smallest necklace strand. Thread the end of the wire through the top loop of the separator and then back through the silver bead and the crimp. Using the pliers, squeeze the crimp closed and trim the excess wire. Repeat with the middle strand and then the lower strand. Attach the strands to the second separator in the same way, making sure that the strands are not crossed.

8 Attach a jump ring to the single ring of the second separator. Thread one end of the clasp through the jump ring and squeeze the clasp gently to close it. Leave the other clasp end open slightly for hooking into the chain.

A Stockingful of Sparkle

Christmas just wouldn't be Christmas without a stocking hanging over the mantelpiece or hung from the bedpost. And this opulent example is fit for a king or queen in shades of regal purple and red, embroidered with gold stars and trimmed with gold beads and a tassel. The design of the stocking has been ingeniously created using the wet-felting method (see pages 14–17). Here, tufts of contrasting fleece have been laid down for the striking diamond pattern and stocking top as part of the felt-making process, to form a single piece of fabric, ready to make up and embellish with ease.

A large star is embroidered with gold thread in the centre of each diamond on the stocking.

Decorative gold beads are sewn in a line across the stocking top.

A gold tassel adds a decorative touch to the top of the stocking.

You will need

- Diamond-patterned homemade felt fabric about 60 x 70cm (24 x 28in) (see page 17), plus strip of synthetic red felt 1.5 x 18cm (⅝ x 7in) • Gold metallic machine embroidery thread • At least 20 gold balls, 2mm (³⁄₃₂in) in diameter • 10 decorative gold beads • 10 gold sequins • 1 gold tassel • Sewing kit (see page 9)

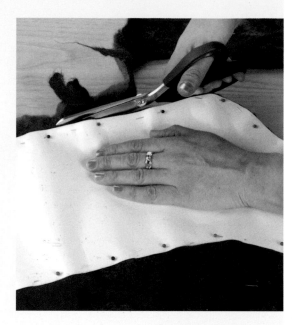

1 Use the template on page 122 to cut out a stocking from paper. Pin the template to the felt, making sure that you have at least 15cm (6in) of the plain red fabric at the top of the stocking shape. Cut around it, keeping close to the paper edge. Remove the pins, turn the template over and pin it back on the fabric, making sure that the bottom of the plain red area is at the same level as on the first stocking piece.

2 Thread the sewing machine and bobbin with gold thread. Machine stitch a line between the darker and paler red diagonal strips on each stocking piece.

Tip
Take your time when machine stitching with the gold thread, as metallic thread can snap quite easily.

3 Thread a needle with a double length of gold thread and embroider a large star (see page 21) in the centre of each diamond on each stocking piece. Work each star individually and knot the thread securely.

4 Thread a needle with a double length of red sewing thread and stitch a gold ball individually onto each intersection of the diagonal red strips. Knot the thread securely.

Tip

When sewing pieces of felt fabric together, adjust the pressure-foot gauge on your sewing machine to '3', to accommodate its bulk (see page 9).

5 With wrong sides facing, pin the stocking pieces together. Starting at one side, just below the plain red stocking top, machine stitch around the stocking, using purple thread and taking a 6mm (¼in) seam allowance, until you reach the same place on the opposite side. Turn the stocking inside out and machine stitch up the remaining open sides. Turn the stocking right side out and fold over the stocking top.

6 Thread a needle with a double length of gold thread and sew decorative gold beads at evenly spaced intervals across the stocking top, just above the scalloped edge, knotting the thread securely. Again with a double length of gold thread, sew a gold sequin in between each of the beads.

7 Fold the strip of red felt over to form a loop and sew it securely to the back of the stocking, on the inside of the stocking top.

8 Using red sewing thread, hand stitch the tassel in place just behind the loop.

Charming Egg Cosies

Wake up every morning to a feast for the eyes with these colourful egg cosies made from insulating wool felt fabric. Each cosy features a different floral motif, two of them cleverly crafted from synthetic felt, with pinched and stitched petals for a naturalistic, 3-D effect. The third cosy design is created from carded fleece using needle felting (see pages 10–12) and decorated with seed beads. Each cosy has a different loop or bobble at the top, so you can choose your favourite type or try all of them. Make an egg cosy for each member of the family and coordinate the colours with your favourite china.

In this design, five felt petals are pinched at the base and sewn together to the cosy front, with a star stitch-embroidered felt circle for the flower centre.

For this variation, four pinched felt petals are sewn in a group onto the cosy front with long star stitches. Decorative French knots are worked between each petal.

Here, white fleece is needle felted to form the petals of a flower with thin strands of pink fleece worked in between. Tiny beads provide further detailing.

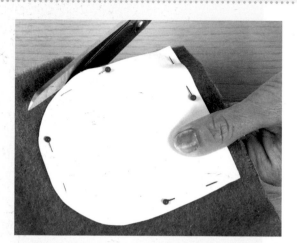

Purple Egg Cosy

1 Use the template on page 123 to cut the egg-cosy shape from paper. For the purple egg cosy, pin the template to purple felt fabric and cut out two pieces for a front and back.

Tip
Enlarge the pattern and make a coordinating teapot cosy using the same needle-felted motifs or felt flowers.

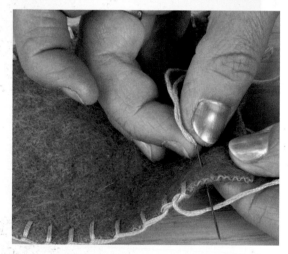

2 Thread a needle with a length of lilac embroidery cotton (floss) and work blanket stitch all the way around the outside edges of each piece (see page 21).

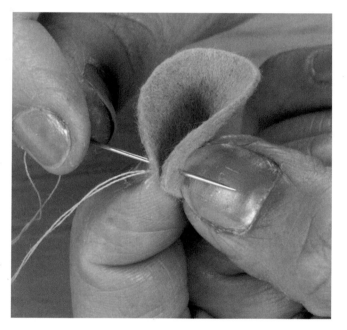

3 Using the template on page 123, cut the lilac petal shape from paper. Pin the template to the lilac felt and cut out a total of five petals. Thread a needle with pink sewing thread. Pinch the base of one petal and secure the pinch in place with a few hand stitches. Repeat with the remaining four petals.

4 Using the pink thread, hand stitch all the petals to the front of the cosy with a few small stitches.

5 Cut out a 1.5cm (½in) circle from the scrap of pink synthetic felt. Thread a needle with three strands of pink embroidery cotton (floss) and sew the circle to the centre of the flower using a star stitch (see page 21).

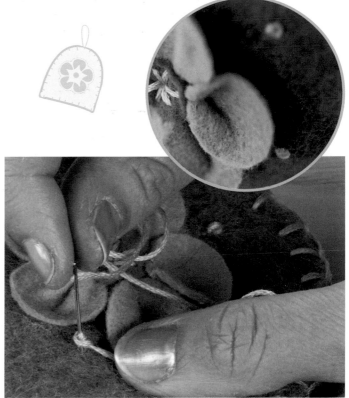

6 Using three strands of pink embroidery cotton (floss), sew French knots in between each of the petals (see page 21), working them individually and knotting the thread before and after each knot.

7 With the wrong sides facing, pin the back and the front pieces of the cosy together around the curved edge and hand stitch using very fine running stitches, keeping as close to the edge as possible.

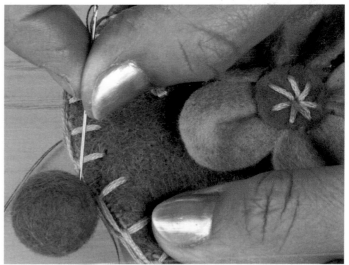

8 Sew the wet-felted ball to the top of the egg cosy, making sure that it is well secured.

Pink Egg Cosy

The pink egg cosy is cut from the same basic pattern as the purple cosy, but the flower on the front is different. It has four petals, which are cut out using the blue petal template on page 123.

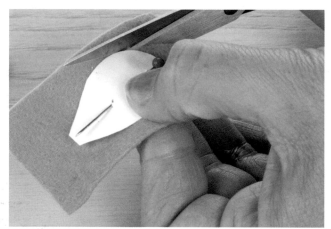

1 Cut two cosy shapes from pink wool felt fabric. Using blue embroidery cotton (floss), stitch all round the edges with blanket stitch, as in Step 2 on page 78. Using the template on page 123, cut the blue petal shape from paper. Pin the template to the blue felt and cut out a total of four petals.

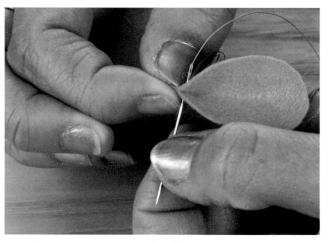

2 Thread a needle with some blue thread. Pinch the base of one petal and secure the pinch in place with a few hand stitches. Repeat with the remaining three petals.

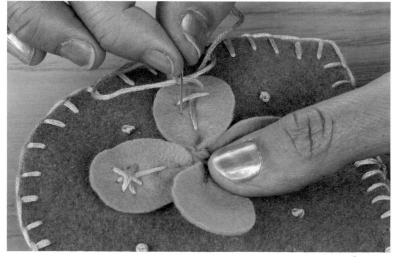

3 Pin the petals to the front of the cosy. Using three strands of blue embroidery cotton (floss), work French knots in between each of the petals (see page 21). Then sew each petal to the cosy with a long star stitch (see page 21), working one longer point to extend down towards the flower centre, as shown. Form the blue ribbon into a loop and tack the ends to the wrong side of the cosy front in the centre of the top curved edge. Pin and stitch the front and back of the cosy together, as in Step 7 on page 79.

Turquoise Egg Cosy

This pretty egg cosy is decorated in a different way, using the very satisfying technique of needle felting. It's ideal if you like the look of embroidery, but find it difficult to achieve a neat finish. Beads add additional sparkle and texture.

1 Cut two cosy shapes from turquoise felt fabric. Using pale pink embroidery cotton (floss), embroider them with blanket stitch (see Step 2 on page 78). Using a marker pen and the cosy template on page 123 as a reference, draw a 12-pointed star on the front of the cosy. Working over a foam block and using a medium-gauge felting needle, needle felt a petal shape over each of the points with white fleece (see page 11), continuing to stab the fleece into the fabric to build up the motif.

2 Lay a thin strip of pink fleece between each of the white petals and needle felt them to build up the pattern as before.

3 Thread a needle with three strands of pale pink embroidery cotton (floss) and work French knots at the end of each of the pink strips. Sew the pink seed beads to the centre of the flower, keeping them as close together as you can. Form the white felt fabric strip into a loop and tack the ends to the wrong side of the cosy front in the centre of the top curved edge. Pin and stitch the front and back of the cosy together, as in Step 7 on page 79.

Mirrored Jewellery Boxes

These citrus-coloured, tactile jewellery boxes would make an eye-catching adornment for any dressing table, or you could use them in the bathroom or guest room for storing small items such as soaps or cotton wool. You could also make larger versions for your make-up and keepsake treasures. The jewellery boxes are quickly created using ready-made, lidded cardboard boxes covered with synthetic felt, then edged with embroidery stitching and decorated with intriguing ornately framed shisha mirrors. Further bead embellishments and sparkling sequins add to the exotic flavour of the East.

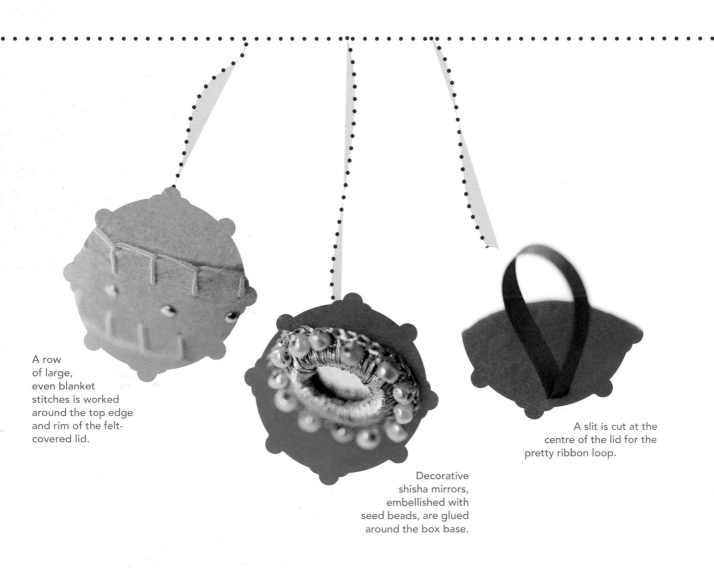

A row of large, even blanket stitches is worked around the top edge and rim of the felt-covered lid.

Decorative shisha mirrors, embellished with seed beads, are glued around the box base.

A slit is cut at the centre of the lid for the pretty ribbon loop.

You will need

• Cardboard boxes with lids – 9cm (3½in) tall and 15cm (6in) in diameter, 10cm (4in) tall and 11cm (4¼in) in diameter and 9cm (3½in) tall and 6.5cm (2½in) in diameter • Synthetic felt, 25cm (10in) square – orange, amber, yellow and dark orange • 1 skein each of six-stranded embroidery cotton (floss) – pink, lime green, green and orange • Shisha mirrors with frames – gold, green and gold bead • Seed beads – opaque pink and green, and transparent green • Decorative sequins – pink and green • 7mm (¼in) wide ribbon – pink, olive green and orange • Decorative nail-head sequins – gold and silver • Wide double-sided tape • PVA (white) glue • Craft knife • Large doll-making needle • Sewing kit (see page 9)

1 Measure the circumference of the base of the 9cm (3½in) tall box and cut a strip of double-sided tape to the same length, allowing an overlap of 1.5cm (½in). Peel away the backing tape from one side of the tape and carefully stick the tape around the box base, butting it up to the rim and overlapping it at the join. Cut another strip the same length and trim the width as necessary, then lay it over the remaining area of the box base.

2 Cut a piece of orange felt 2cm (¾in) wider than the overall width of the box base and 2cm (¾in) longer than the overall length. Remove the remaining backing from the tape and carefully lay the felt onto the box base, butting one long edge of the felt up to the rim. Mark and trim the end of the felt to achieve an exact, neat join, then run over the surface of the felt with your fingers to create a smooth finish. Using small embroidery scissors, cut away the excess around the bottom edge of the box. Cover the side of the box lid with orange felt in the same way.

3 Place the lid, top down, on orange felt and draw around it with a fade-away marker. Removing the backing, cover the back of the felt circle with strips of double-sided tape, overlapping the circle slightly. Use embroidery scissors to cut out the circle, then peel away the remaining backing and stick the felt onto the lid, smoothing over the surface as in Step 2. Cover the bottom of the box base in the same way.

4 Measure 1cm (³/₈in) from the top edge of the lid and, using the fade-away marker, draw a series of dots spaced 5mm (¼in) apart all the way around the side of the lid, then corresponding dots on the top edge of the lid. Thread a needle with three strands of pink embroidery cotton (floss) and blanket stitch around the top of the lid (see page 21), using the marker points as a guide. Repeat around the rim of the lid in the same way.

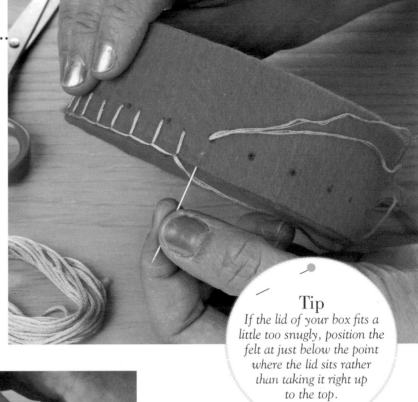

Tip
If the lid of your box fits a little too snugly, position the felt at just below the point where the lid sits rather than taking it right up to the top.

5 Thread a needle with pink thread and sew about ten pink seed beads around the edge of at least ten gold shisha mirrors, knotting the thread securely. Using the marker, mark ten equally spaced points around the centre of the box side. Use a cocktail stick to apply a large dot of glue to the back of each mirror and stick in place over the marks. Apply a little dot of glue in between each mirror and stick on a pink sequin.

6 Make a small incision at the centre of the lid with a craft knife. Thread both ends of a 15cm (6in) length of pink ribbon through a large doll-making needle, then pass the needle through the hole in the lid, tie the ribbon ends in a knot and trim the excess. Decorate the side of the lid by gluing on a series of evenly spaced gold nail-head sequins. Cover the other boxes in the same way, using the other felt and embellishment colours, and referring to the main photograph on page 83 for the positioning of the mirrors and sequins.

Tropical Tote Bag

This fruit-themed tote bag will brighten up summer days and banish the winter blues. It is big enough to take shopping or roomy enough to use on the beach. The sumptuous colours have been achieved by dying white wool fabric in vibrant citrus shades of lime, yellow and orange (see page 7). The stylized, retro-style fruit motifs are easily cut from the felt fabric, using the templates provided, then artfully embellished with embroidery and beads, and simply attached to the bag with fabric glue – or see page 91 for an alternative version. A clever clasp, made from felt strips, provides an additional novelty feature.

Two pineapple motifs cut from yellow dyed felt are embellished with embroidered backstitches and seed beads.

Orange slice motifs cut from orange dyed felt fabric are embroidered with orange seed beads for pips.

A clever fastener is fashioned out of two strips of coloured felt.

You will need

• Lime green dyed wool felt fabric (see page 7), 30 x 41cm (12 x 16in) • Pale lime green dyed wool felt fabric (see page 7), 70 x 50cm (28 x 20in) • Yellow dyed wool felt fabric (see page 7), 30cm (12in) square • Scraps of orange dyed wool felt fabric (see page 7) • 0.5m (½yd) of coordinating lining fabric • 1 skein each of six-stranded embroidery cotton (floss) – dark green, pale green and orange • Seed beads – green and orange • 10 green crystal beads • Fabric glue and plastic spreader • Sewing kit (see page 9)

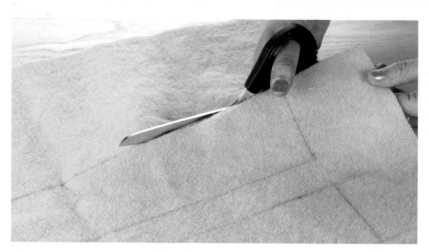

1 Using a fade-away marker, measure and mark out on the lime green felt fabric two bag sides 36 x 7cm (14¼ x 2¾in) and a bag base 7 x 32cm (2¾ x 12½in), then cut out. Measure and mark out on the pale lime green felt fabric a bag front and back 36 x 32cm (14¼ x 12½in), then cut out.

Tip
Cut out the inner areas of the motif first before cutting around the outline of the template.

2 Using the template on page 123, cut out the pineapple motif from paper, carefully cutting out the inner areas of the design with embroidery scissors. Pin the template to the yellow felt fabric and carefully cut out the motif – take time and cut carefully, as any imperfections will show up on your finished bag. Cut out a second pineapple in the same way.

3 Thread a needle with three strands of dark green embroidery cotton (floss) and work backstitches (see page 20) in a 'V' shape below the bottom half of each cutout diamond. Stitch a green seed bead at the base of the 'V'. Work both pineapples in the same way, but use pale green embroidery cotton (floss) for the second motif. Sew a green crystal bead to the tips of the top five leaves of each pineapple.

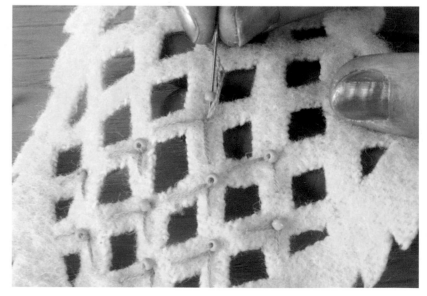

4 Using the template on page 123, cut out the solid orange slice from paper. Pin the template to the orange felt fabric and cut out with pinking shears. Using three strands of orange embroidery cotton (floss), work running stitch around the edge, then work the lines shown on the printed template with backstitch (see page 20). Sew orange seed beads randomly over the motif to represent pips. Cut out and work a second orange slice in the same way, plus a half orange slice (see page 123 for the template). Using the template on page 123, cut out a segmented orange slice from paper, cutting out the inner sections with embroidery scissors. Cut two segmented slices from the orange felt and decorate with rows of orange seed beads between the segments.

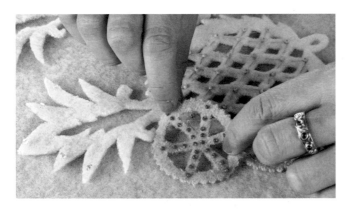

5 Arrange the motifs on the bag front. Pour a little of the fabric glue into a tray and, using a plastic spreader, spread the adhesive over the back of the motifs, making sure that the glue is taken right to the edges. Lay them on the bag and gently press them down with your fingers so that the pieces make good contact with the base fabric.

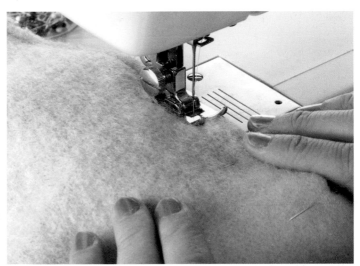

6 With right sides facing, pin the bag front to one of the bag sides and machine stitch together, taking in a 6mm (¼in) seam allowance. Pin the bag back to the remaining side and machine stitch in the same way. With right sides facing, pin the back and side to the front and side and machine stitch together as before. Pin the bag base to the bottom of the bag and machine stitch as before, taking your time as you do so to ensure that it fits well. Turn the bag right side out.

7 Using a fade-away marker, measure and mark out on the lining fabric two sides 38 x 7cm (15 x 2¾in), a base 7 x 32cm (2¾in x 12½in) and a front and back 38 x 32cm (15 x 12½in), then cut out. With right sides facing, pin and machine stitch the lining together, as for the bag.

8 Cut two long strips 5 x 56cm (2 x 22in) from the pale lime green felt fabric and roll up to form two long tubes. Pin, then stitch the open edge closed with small, neat slipstitches. Measure 6.5cm (2½in) from each side along the top edge of the front and back of the bag and hand stitch the ends of each handle in place.

Tip
Use long pins with ball ends to ensure that you don't lose your pins in the felt.

9 Cut a 1.5 x 22cm (¾ x 8¾in) strip of yellow felt fabric. Roll it up into a tube. Pin, then stitch the open edge closed with small, neat slipstitches. Form the tube into a loop and hand stitch the ends together for 8.5cm (3¼in), as shown. Hand stitch securely to the centre inside back edge of the bag.

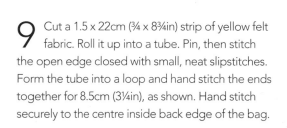

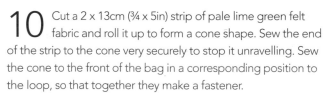

10 Cut a 2 x 13cm (¾ x 5in) strip of pale lime green felt fabric and roll it up to form a cone shape. Sew the end of the strip to the cone very securely to stop it unravelling. Sew the cone to the front of the bag in a corresponding position to the loop, so that together they make a fastener.

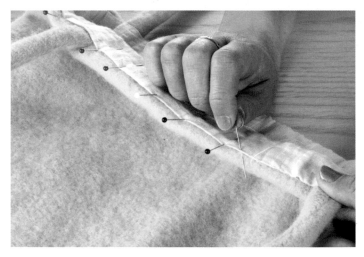

11 Turn over and press down a 2cm (¾in) hem all the way around the top edge of the lining. Push the lining into the bag and pin it to the bag just below the top edge. Hand stitch in place using 'invisible' slipstitches (see page 9).

Snowflake Tote Bag

This stylish winter-themed tote bag is made in the same way as the Tropical Tote Bag, but using an appropriately cooler colour scheme and featuring festive snowflake and circle motifs.

Cut the front and back of the bag from pale lilac dyed wool felt fabric, the sides and base from turquoise, the strips for the loop and cone fastening from aqua and green respectively and the handles from aqua. Cut each of the two different designs of snowflake – see page 124 for templates – twice from green and turquoise, and aqua and pale green felt, together with circles of varying sizes from the range of felt fabrics used. As with the fruit motifs for the tropical bag, the snowflakes can then be embroidered with backstitches and embellished with beads, as shown. Layer the felt circles and embroider them with intersecting lines. Arrange the motifs and glue them in place on the bag front, and then make up the bag and lining in the same way as for the Tropical Tote Bag.

Fabulous Flower Corsages

These attractive blooms – a cheerful yellow daffodil to herald spring and a dahlia in autumn shades of red, rust and orange – would look stunning adorning any jacket or coat, and could be easily adapted to make alternative blooms suitable for summer and winter – see the rose corsage on page 95. The dahlia is quickly created by layering circles of homemade felt fabric in varying colours, trimmed into petal shapes and shaded with needle felting (see pages 10–12). The central trumpet of the felt daffodil is cleverly formed from wet-felted fleece (see page 18) and embellished with glass beads.

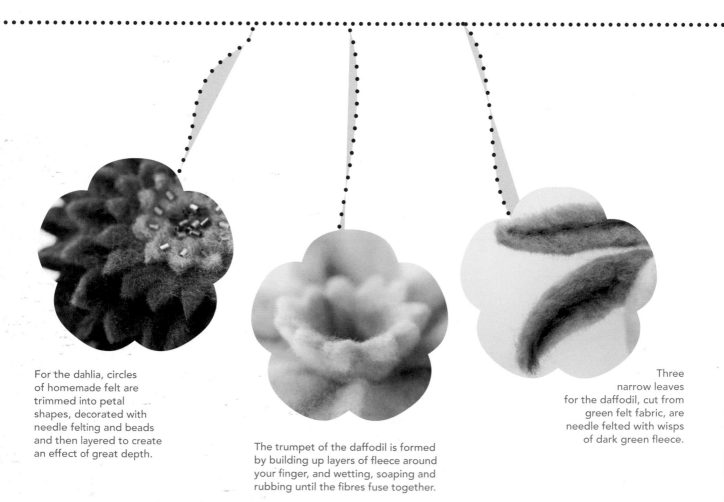

For the dahlia, circles of homemade felt are trimmed into petal shapes, decorated with needle felting and beads and then layered to create an effect of great depth.

The trumpet of the daffodil is formed by building up layers of fleece around your finger, and wetting, soaping and rubbing until the fibres fuse together.

Three narrow leaves for the daffodil, cut from green felt fabric, are needle felted with wisps of dark green fleece.

Dahlia corsage

1 Using a compass, draw four circles on a piece of paper 2.5cm (1in), 3.5cm (1⅜in), 4cm (1½in) and 10cm (4in) in diameter, then cut out. Pin the smallest circle template to the orange felt and carefully cut out. Pin the next two larger circle templates to the rust felt and the largest circle template to the dark red felt, then cut out.

2 Using small embroidery scissors, carefully snip all the way around the outer edge of each felt circle to create the petals of the flower.

3 Working over a foam block, pull off wisps of the red fleece. Using a fine-gauge felting needle, needle felt the red fleece along every petal on the outer portion of the largest rust felt flower (see page 12). Then needle felt the rust fleece on alternate petals of the outer portion of the dark red felt flower.

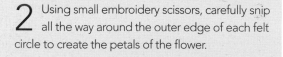

4 Using orange thread, sew a mixture of red and white rocaille beads to the centre of the orange felt flower. Layer the circles in size order with the smallest on the top and stitch them together through the centre.

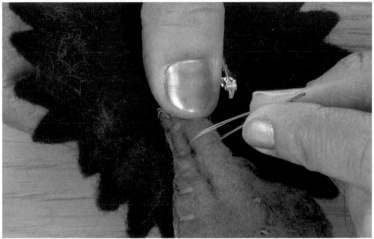

5 Turn the flower over to the back. Using a double length of thread, sew a pin brooch centrally in place, making sure that it is well secured.

6 Using the template on page 124, cut out a dahlia leaf from paper. Pin to the emerald green felt fabric and cut out three leaves. Using the green embroidery cotton (floss), work running stitch through the centre of the leaves and blanket stitch around the outer edges (see pages 20–21). Pinch the leaves at the pointed tip end and secure the pinch in place with a few stitches. Sew two leaves together to the back of the flower on one side and the other leaf on the opposite side.

Rose Corsage

This beautiful full-blown rose corsage is made in a similar way to the dahlia corsage. Use it on a lapel or pin it to a felt hat (see page 52) or bag (see page 34).

Cut two 6 x 30cm (2¼ x 12in) strips of homemade red felt, one in a darker shade and one in a paler shade; cut in half widthways. Stitch one long edge and both ends of each piece with blanket stitch (see page 21), using paler red embroidery cotton (floss) for the darker felt and vice versa. Roll up one pale strip and stitch at the non-embroidered base, then wrap with a darker strip and secure at the base. Wrap with the other strips to complete the rose, then stitch red seed beads and red and white glass rocailles around the petals. Using the template on page 124, cut two rose leaves from green felt and embroider as in Step 6 above (without pinching), then sew in place. Attach the brooch pin.

Daffodil corsage

1 Using the template on page 124, cut out a daffodil petal from paper. Pin the template to the yellow felt fabric and cut out five petals.

> **Tip**
> *When making the yellow felt (see pages 15–16), add a few wisps of orange fleece to the yellow, to add a little colour variation, then make sure you incorporate some of this variation when cutting out the petals.*

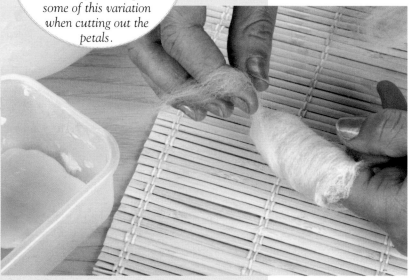

2 Wrap a little orange fleece around your finger, adding wisps of yellow, until it is covered. Wet with warm water, soap and rub gently until the fibres no longer move around. Build up the layers with thin strips of white fleece. Ease the tube off your finger and cover the end with some more wisps of yellow and white fleece. Wet, soap and rub as before until the fibres no longer move.

3 Rinse the felt in water. Place a piece of scrunched-up kitchen foil into the fleece tube and roll up in a bamboo mat. Roll backwards and forwards until the fleece has thickened. Shock the fleece in hot and then cold water while continuing to roll it until it has felted and shrunk to the desired size. Leave the felt to dry.

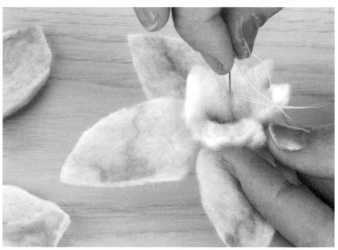

4 Using small embroidery scissors, trim the tube to size, then carefully cut a zigzag around the top to give shape to the flower.

5 Thread a needle with a double length of yellow thread and assemble the daffodil by sewing each of the petals to the underside of the central trumpet.

6 Sew a few white and green rocaille beads to the centre of the flower, then sew the brooch pin to the centre back of the corsage, making sure that it is well secured.

7 Using the template on page 124, cut a daffodil leaf from paper. Pin the template to the grass green felt fabric and cut out three leaves. Use the felting needle to needle felt a wisp of dark green fleece down the centre of each leaf (see page 12). Attach the leaves to the back of the corsage using a double length of thread.

Christening Booties and Rattle

This charming christening set in shades of pastel pink and yellow is irresistible and would make a welcome gift for a new baby girl or can be adapted for a boy (see page 105). The invitingly soft rattle is easily needle felted around a polystyrene former (see page 13), then trimmed with matching ribbon and wet-felted balls (see page 16). Both dainty booties are ingeniously created as one piece using the traditional wet-felting technique and a special double template (see page 18), and incorporate a contrasting colour on the inside, which is revealed in a decorative cutaway.

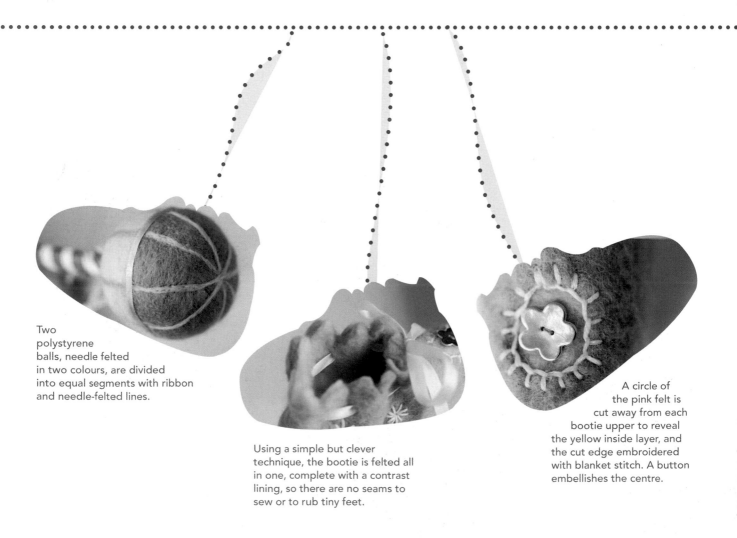

Two polystyrene balls, needle felted in two colours, are divided into equal segments with ribbon and needle-felted lines.

Using a simple but clever technique, the bootie is felted all in one, complete with a contrast lining, so there are no seams to sew or to rub tiny feet.

A circle of the pink felt is cut away from each bootie upper to reveal the yellow inside layer, and the cut edge embroidered with blanket stitch. A button embellishes the centre.

Rattle

1 Wrap a length of yellow fleece around a polystyrene ball, following the line of the seam around the middle of the former. Repeatedly stab one area with a medium-gauge multi-needle felting tool until the fleece no longer comes away from the ball. Continue wrapping and stabbing until that half of the ball is covered with fleece and it has thickened and become felted.

2 Wrap a length of pink fleece around the other half of the ball, butting it up against the yellow fleece, and needle felt in the same way until the ball has been densely covered and well felted. Work the other ball in the same way.

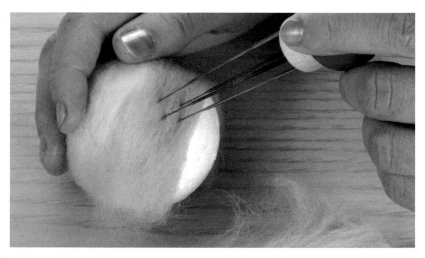

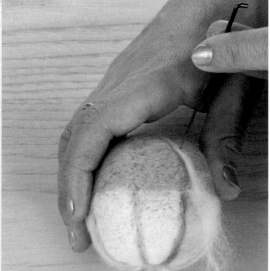

3 Along the middle line of the ball, where the two colours meet, mark a series of points 2.5cm (1in) apart with a fade-away marker. Pull off a thin length of pink fleece. Starting at one mark, push the fleece into the ball using a fine-gauge felting needle. Continue to work the fleece up to and over the top of the yellow half of the ball until you meet the pen mark on the opposite side. Work lines of pink fleece to join the remaining marks, then work lines in yellow fleece over the pink half of the ball in the same way. Repeat with the second polystyrene ball.

4 Pour a little PVA (white) glue into a tray. Using a cocktail stick, run a fine line of the glue around the middle of one ball. Cut a 20cm (8in) length of pink ribbon and accurately lay it along the line of adhesive. Gently run your finger over the ribbon to make sure that it has made contact with the glue. Repeat for the second ball.

5 Using a pencil, draw a spiral along the length of the dowel, then draw a line parallel to the first line 5mm (¼in) away. Paint every alternate section with yellow paint, keeping as close to the pencil lines as possible. Leave to dry, then paint the remaining sections with pink paint. Apply at least two coats of paint so that the wood beneath doesn't show.

Tip
When painting the wooden dowel, make sure that you use a non-toxic paint that is suitable for babies' toys.

6 Using the darning needle, thread each pink wet-felted ball onto an 11cm (4¼in) length of yellow ribbon, then thread each yellow wet-felted ball onto an 11cm (4¼in) length of pink ribbon, securing each of the ends below the balls with a knot. Attach the ends of all four ribbons to the end of the dowel with a couple of strips of adhesive tape.

7 Using the extra piece of dowel, make a hole about 2.5cm (1in) deep in the top of the yellow half of each polystyrene ball. Mix up the two parts of the epoxy resin following the manufacturer's instructions and cover one end of the painted dowel generously with the glue. Push the end into the hole of one polystyrene ball and leave it set for ten minutes. Repeat with the other end of the dowel and the other polystyrene ball.

Booties

✂

You will need
- 30g (1oz) of carded fleece – pastel yellow and pink • 1 skein of yellow six-stranded embroidery cotton (floss)
- 2 silver flower buttons • 1m (1yd) of 6mm (¼in) wide yellow ribbon • A4 (US letter) sheet of thin plastic
- Adhesive tape • Wet-felting equipment (see page 14) • Bubble wrap • Leather punch • Sewing kit (see page 9)

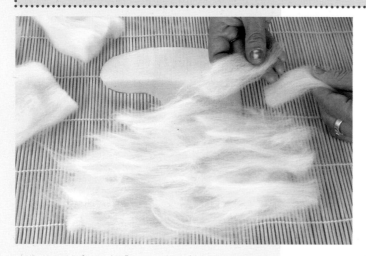

1 Using the template on page 125, cut out the bootie shape from paper. Lay the paper template over the sheet of plastic and secure with adhesive tape. Using a marker, carefully draw around the template, then cut out the bootie from the plastic with scissors, keeping as close to the pen marks as possible (see page 18). Place the template on the bamboo blind. Cut off pieces of yellow fleece measuring no longer than about 9cm (3½in). Pull the pieces of fleece into tufts and lay them vertically across the template, overlapping rows and the sides of the template. Continue until the template has been completely covered.

2 Cover the fleece with a piece of net curtain and wet well with warm water. Rub over the surface with a bar of soap, then continue rubbing with your hands until the fibres no longer move (see Step 4, page 15). Turn the template over and fold in the excess fleece. Lay down another layer of yellow fleece in the same vertical direction as before and with an overlap at the sides. Cover with net curtain, then wet, soap and rub as before until the fibres no longer move.

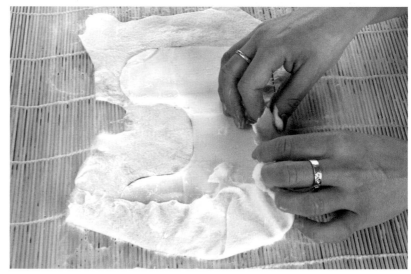

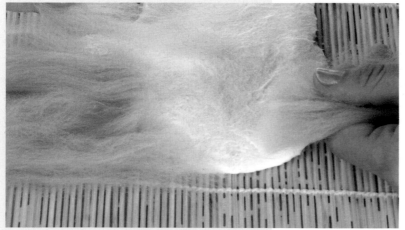

3 Turn the template back over to the original side and fold in the excess fleece. Cover horizontally with tufts of pink fleece, then wet, soap and rub, as in Step 2. Turn the template over and repeat on the other side. Then turn the template over again and lay down a final layer of pink fleece, but this time vertically and without overlapping the template; just ensure that the fleece is dense and that the colour change beneath doesn't show through the pink. Turn the template over and repeat on the other side.

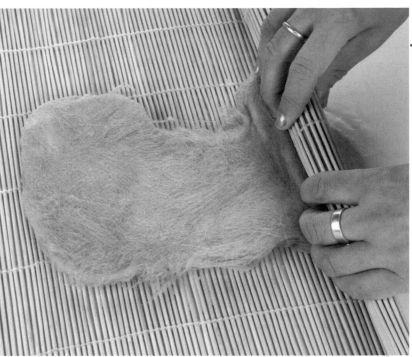

4 Once you are certain that the fibres no longer move, carefully transfer the fleece to a bowl and rinse it in warm water to remove the soap, taking care, as the fleece is still very delicate at this stage. Gently squeeze out any excess water.

5 Roll up the booties tightly in the bamboo blind and roll backwards and forwards. Check them every ten minutes and turn them periodically so that they shrink and felt evenly. Wearing rubber gloves, shock the booties by plunging them into hot water and then cold water. Repeat the rolling process until the felt has thickened.

6 Snip the bootie shape down the centre and gently pull out the template. Roll up in the blind and roll backwards and forwards for another ten minutes, turning periodically as you do so. Shock the booties again in hot and cold water, then continue rolling until they are well felted and have shrunk to the desired size. Rinse the booties to remove all the soap, stuff with bubble wrap and leave in a warm place overnight to dry.

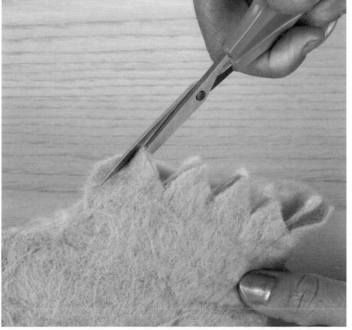

7 Using small embroidery scissors, cut a neat little zigzag around the opening of each of the booties.

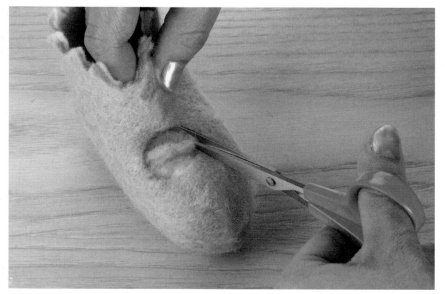

8 Using a fade-away marker, draw a 2cm (¾in) circle on the front of the upper of one bootie. Using the embroidery scissors, carefully snip away the pink felt to reveal the yellow felt beneath – as you make your first snips, you will be able to see clearly the colour change between the two layers. Cut out the design on the other bootie in the same way.

9 Thread a needle with a length of yellow embroidery cotton (floss) and work blanket stitch around the cut edge of the circle on each bootie (see page 21). Thread a needle with a double length of yellow thread and sew a button in the centre of each of the circle motifs, making sure that each one is well secured.

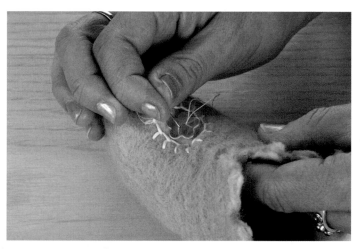

10 Using a fade-away marker, mark about 11 dots over each bootie, keeping them evenly spaced. Work a neat flower stitch over each mark (see page 21), knotting the thread before and after each one has been worked.

11 Mark a series of ten evenly spaced points around the top of each bootie. Using a leather punch, punch out a hole at each of the points. Repeat with the other bootie.

12 Cut the length of ribbon in half. Thread a darning needle with one half and thread it through the holes, starting with the left-hand hole at the front and working clockwise around the bootie until all the holes have been threaded. Pull the ribbon, tie in a bow and trim the ends to length. Repeat with the other bootie.

Baby Boy Booties

These handsome little booties are made in exactly the same way as the baby girl booties, but the colour scheme has been changed to suit a baby boy.

Use fleece in shades of baby blue and soft lilac for the boot and integral lining, following the instructions for the girl's booties. Work the blanket-stitch edging around the cutout circle in matching blue embroidery cotton (floss), and instead of using a flower button at the centre, use a star. Alternatively, you could coordinate the colours with a christening outfit or the overall scheme of the occasion – ivory is traditional, but most pastel shades will work well for either a girl or a boy.

Quick Appliqué Cushion

Relax at home in comfort and style with this characterful cushion featuring a bold appliquéd design worked in pretty floral prints onto a richly coloured dyed wool felt fabric. The bird in the centre is a symbol of freedom and the spirit, but you could choose any motif you like. Gold fringing, pearl beads and sequins have also been incorporated to add extra interest and sparkle. For ease and speed, bonding web (see page 9) is used to attach the motifs to the cushion cover, requiring only a hot iron to secure them in place, rather than extensive hemming and hand sewing.

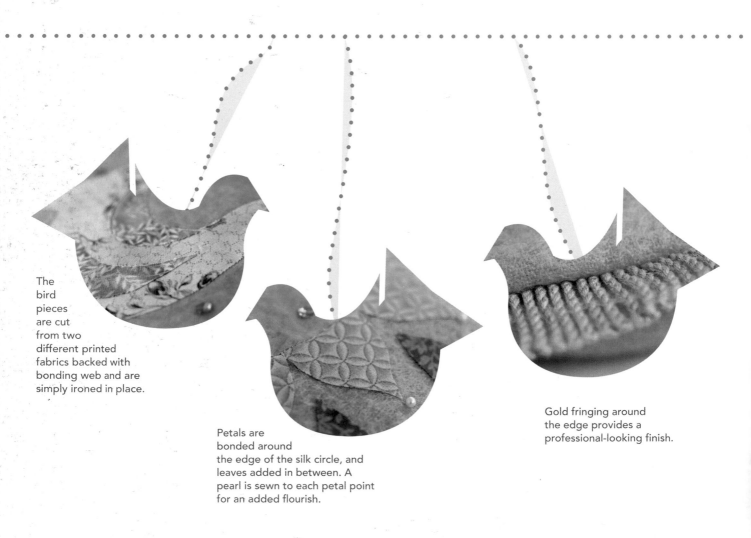

The bird pieces are cut from two different printed fabrics backed with bonding web and are simply ironed in place.

Petals are bonded around the edge of the silk circle, and leaves added in between. A pearl is sewn to each petal point for an added flourish.

Gold fringing around the edge provides a professional-looking finish.

1 Using a fade-away marker, draw a 40cm (16in) square onto the orange felt fabric for the cushion cover front. For the back sections, draw one rectangle 40 x 27cm (16 x 10½in) and another 40 x 32cm (16 x 12½in).

Tip
Choose printed fabrics that are all in the same colour range, and that contrast with the felt, so that your appliqué design will show up clearly against the background colour.

2 Using a hot iron, iron the bonding web onto the back of each of the squares of patterned fabric and the silk fabric, making sure that the latter are slightly larger than the bonding web (see page 9).

3 Using the templates on page 125, cut out a petal and a leaf from thin paper or tracing paper. Cut out the bird body, without the back wing (at the top), as one template, then the back wing and front wing as two separate templates. Pin the petal template to one of the patterned fabrics and carefully cut around it. Cut a total of 14 petals. Cut 14 leaves from a different patterned fabric.

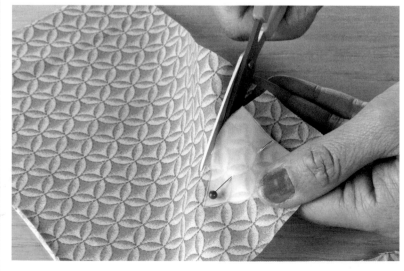

4 Pin the bird body template to another patterned fabric and carefully cut around the motif, keeping as close to the edge of the template as possible. Cut out the back and front wings from another patterned fabric. Fuse bonding web onto the back of the silk fabric as in Step 2. Using a compass, draw an 18cm (7in) diameter circle onto the back of the silk and cut it out.

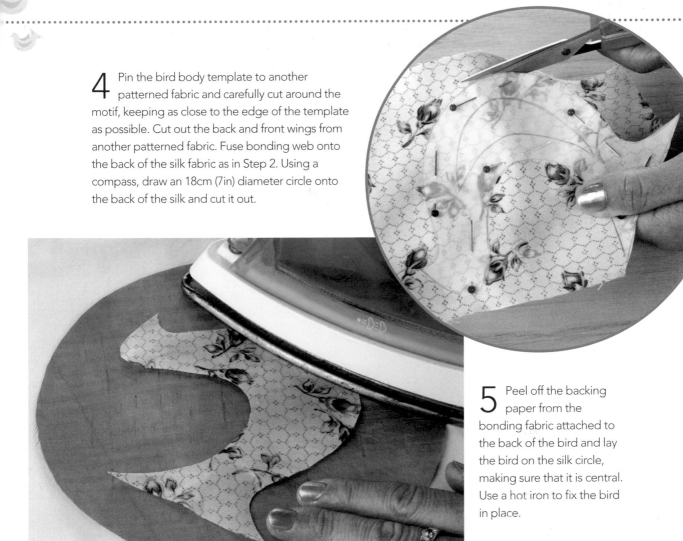

5 Peel off the backing paper from the bonding fabric attached to the back of the bird and lay the bird on the silk circle, making sure that it is central. Use a hot iron to fix the bird in place.

6 Remove the backing paper from the bonding paper attached to the wings, place in position on the bird and fix with the iron, as in Step 5.

7 Peel off the backing paper from the silk circle and lay it in the centre of the cushion cover front. Use the iron to fix it in place, keeping the heat and the pressure evenly distributed as you do so. Attach the petals in the same way, laying them slightly over the silk circle, so that the corners of the petals touch one another. Lay the leaves in between the petals, fixing each one in place before moving on to the next.

Tip
Lay the motifs down and arrange them on the cushion cover before ironing them into their final position.

8 Using a fade-away marker, randomly mark about 14 points over the silk background. Thread a needle with a length of blue thread and sew on a sequin at each point, knotting the thread securely.

9 Thread a needle with a length of white thread and sew a seed pearl to the point of each petal, knotting the thread securely each time.

10 With the front cover right side up, accurately pin the fringing around the inside edge of the fabric, with the fringing laying over the fabric. Carefully machine stitch in place, taking time to achieve a neat finish.

Tip
You may find it easier to tack (baste) the fringing in place at this stage – it will be stitched in position when the side seams are sewn in Step 12.

11 Fold over and pin down 2cm (¾in) along one long edge of each back cover piece and machine stitch in place.

12 With the right sides facing, lay the slightly narrower back section over the front cover, then lay down the wider section next to it, overlapping by 15cm (6in) along the hemmed edges and aligning the sides. Pin the layers together, then machine stitch, taking a 6mm (¼in) seam allowance and making sure that the fringing is all facing inwards so that the ends don't get caught in the seam. Turn the cover right side out and insert the cushion pad.

This stylized bird motif is brought to life by cutting the body and wings from different interestingly patterned fabrics and setting it against a plain silk background for contrast, decoratively framed with yet another toning printed fabric. But first the fabrics are backed with bonding web, so that the different elements of the design can be quickly built up by simply laying one piece over the other and ironing them into place, as well as onto the cushion cover. Light-catching, jewel-like sequins – one used for the bird's eye – and dainty seed pearls add an extra richness to the surface.

Jester-Style Slippers

Snuggle up this winter in these cosy, fun-shaped slippers in bright colours, scattered with funky polka dots. The instructions on the following pages will make a UK size 4 or US size 6 slipper, but the pattern can be scaled up for bigger feet or down for smaller ones. Each slipper is made from wet-felted strips of carded fleece (see pages 14–18) using a shaped template that eliminates the need for seams, so they are easy to make and comfortable to wear. The decorative dots are added using needle-felting (see page 12) and embellished with light-catching sequins. Small wet-felted balls (see page 16) add a comic finishing touch.

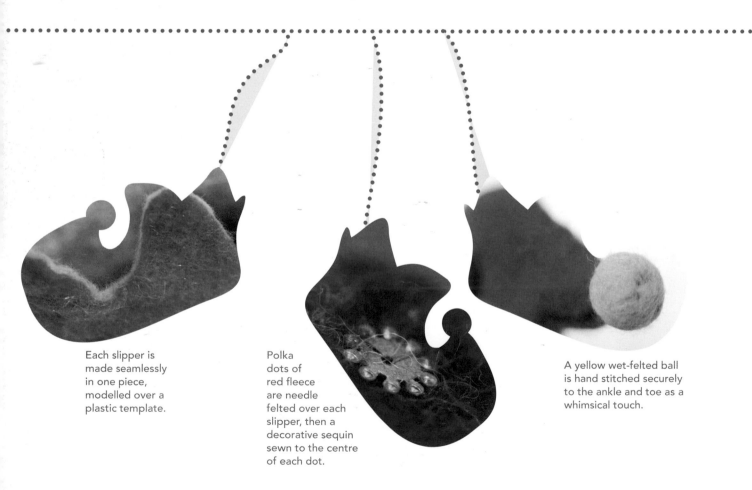

Each slipper is made seamlessly in one piece, modelled over a plastic template.

Polka dots of red fleece are needle felted over each slipper, then a decorative sequin sewn to the centre of each dot.

A yellow wet-felted ball is hand stitched securely to the ankle and toe as a whimsical touch.

You will need

• 50g (1¾oz) of carded fleece – bright yellow and orange • Small amount of red carded fleece • Pink sparkle Angelina fibres (see page 7) • About 40 red decorative sequins • 4 yellow wet-felted balls (see page 16), about 3cm (1¼in) in diameter • A4 (US letter) sheet of thin plastic • Adhesive tape • Wet-felting equipment (see page 14) • Bubble wrap • Needle-felting equipment (see page 10) • Sewing kit (see page 9)

1 Enlarge the slipper template on page 126 on a photocopier until it fits around your own foot comfortably, allowing an extra 1.5cm (½in) all round, then enlarge by a further 20% to allow for shrinkage (the enlargement specified will make a UK size 4 or US size 6 slipper). Cut the slipper shape from paper. Lay the paper template over the sheet of plastic and secure with adhesive tape. Using a marker, carefully draw around the template, then accurately cut out the slipper from the plastic. Place the template on a bamboo blind. Pinch off tufts of the yellow fleece about 10cm (4in) long and lay them vertically over the template, overlapping rows and the sides of the template. Continue until the template has been completely covered.

Tip
Remember that the first colour of fleece that you lay down will become the inside of your slippers.

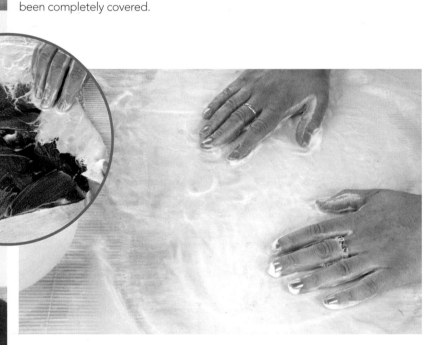

2 Continue as in Steps 2–5 on pages 102–103 using orange fleece for the second layer, to which you can add a scattering of pink Angelina fibres for a sparkling effect. Repeat to make a second slipper.

3 Using scissors, snip across the top of each slipper and gently ease out the template. Wearing rubber gloves, shock the felt by plunging it into hot water and then cold water. Repeat the rolling and shocking process until the felt has hardened, thickened and shrunk to the desired size. Stuff the slippers with bubble wrap and leave in a warm place overnight to dry.

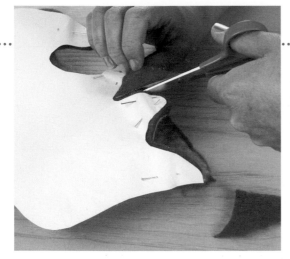

4 Using the template on page 126, cut out the fancy-edged slipper design from paper. Pin it to one side of a slipper. Carefully cut out the shape, then transfer the template to the other side and cut out, keeping the two sides symmetrical. Repeat with the second slipper.

5 Pinch out a small wad of red fleece. Using the fancy-edged slipper design template on page 126 for reference, needle felt polka dots, about 2cm (¾in) in diameter, over both the slippers with a medium-gauge felting needle (see page 12). Make sure you don't needle felt the two sides of the slipper together.

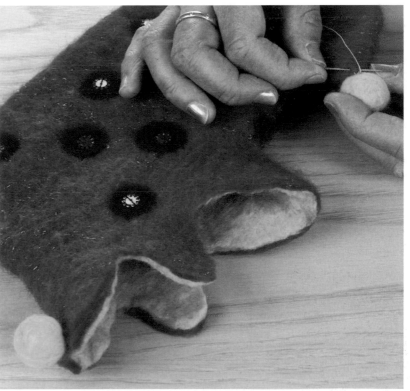

6 Sew a decorative sequin to the centre of each polka dot, working each sequin individually and knotting the thread securely.

7 Use yellow thread to hand stitch a yellow wet-felted ball securely to the ankle and toe of each slipper to finish.

Templates

All of the templates required for the projects in this book are to be found here. Most of these are printed full size, but a few need to be enlarged on a photocopier at the percentage specified.

❄ Glittering Tree Decorations, pages 26–29 ❄

Bell

Tree

Star

Snowflake

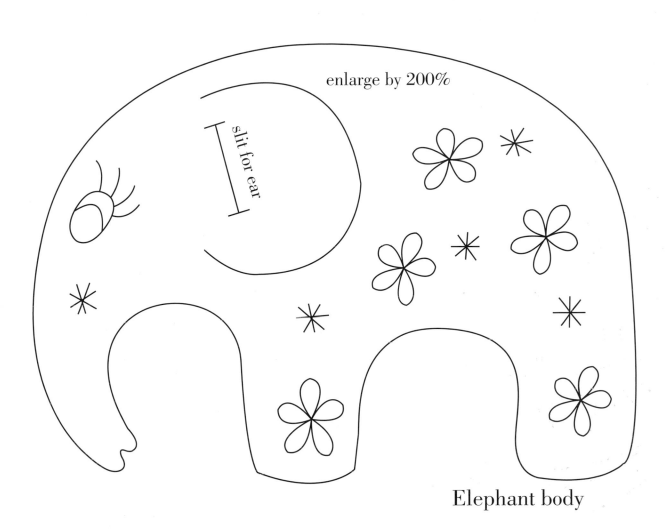

enlarge by 200%

slit for ear

Elephant body

Using the templates

Trace over the design onto tracing paper with a soft pencil, turn the tracing over and scribble over the lines of the design with a pencil, then turn the tracing back to the right side, attach to a piece of paper with masking tape and redraw the lines to transfer the motif. If the template is going to be used more than just a few times, it is advisable to transfer it onto thin card, which is more durable than paper. See page 18 for instructions on cutting out and using a plastic double template.

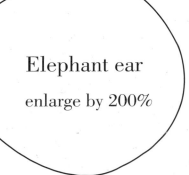

Elephant ear

enlarge by 200%

Favourite Jumper Bag, pages 34–38

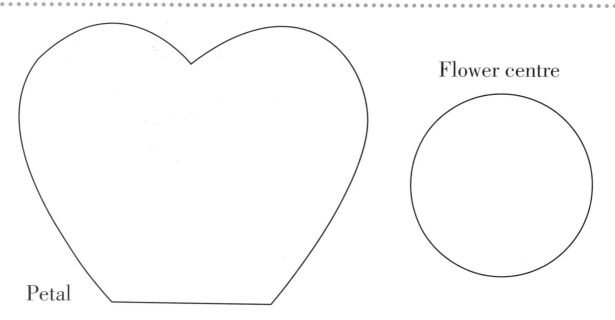

Flower centre

Petal

 ## Paisley Purse, pages 40–45

Teardrop shapes

Beautiful Bird Mobile, pages 46–51

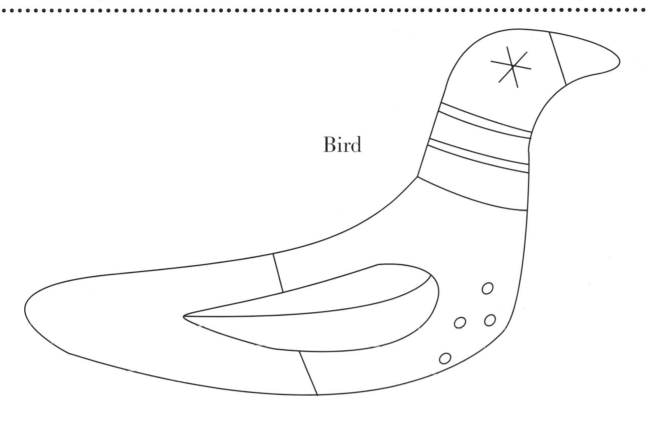

Bird

 ## Rustic Beret, pages 52–55

Small oak leaf

Large oak leaf

A

B

C

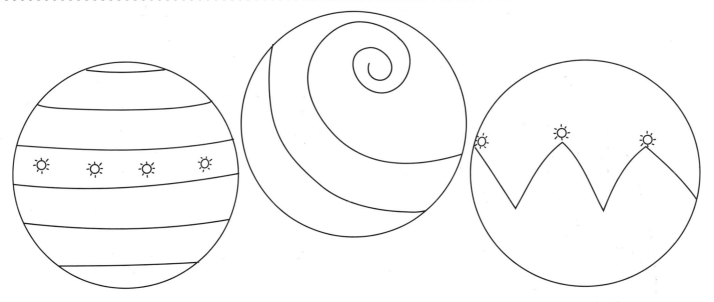

 Vibrant Document Bag, pages 62–67

enlarge by 200%

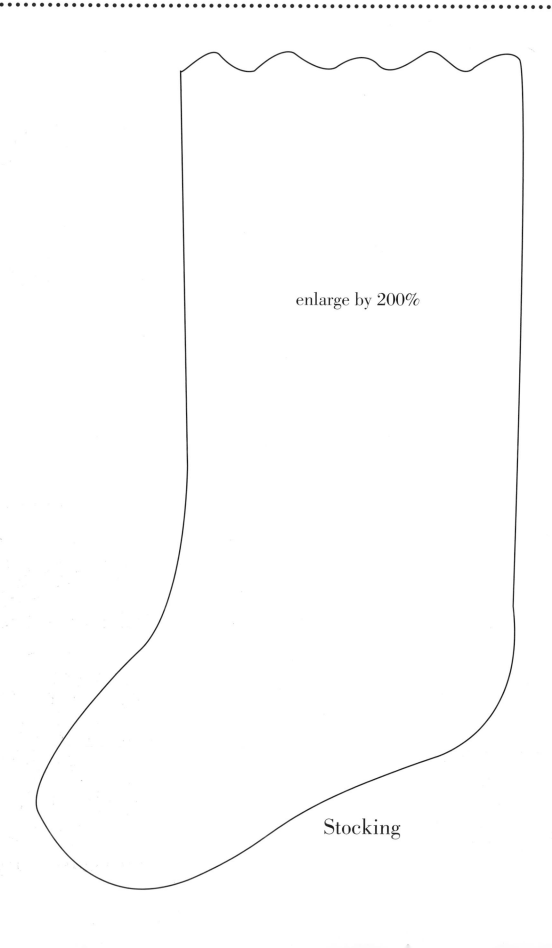

enlarge by 200%

Stocking

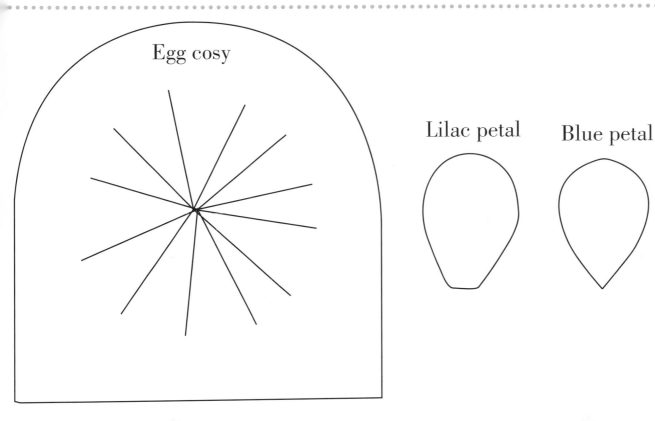

Egg cosy

Lilac petal

Blue petal

Tropical Tote Bag, page 86–90

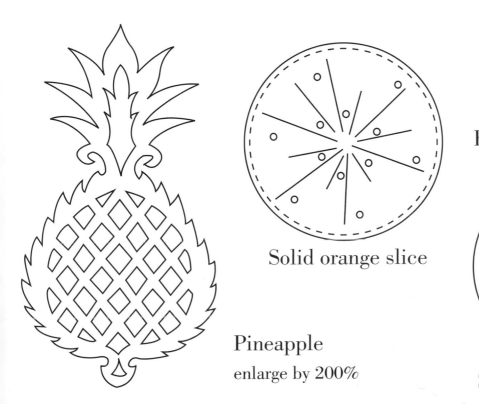

Solid orange slice

Pineapple
enlarge by 200%

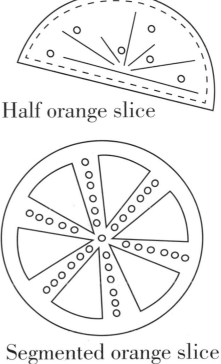

Half orange slice

Segmented orange slice

Snowflakes

 Fabulous Flower Corsages, pages 92–97

Daffodil petal

Dahlia & rose leaf

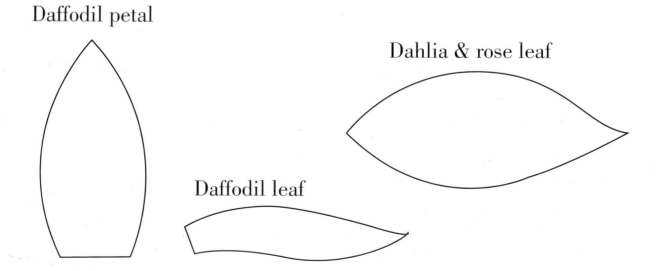

Daffodil leaf

Christening Booties, page 98–105

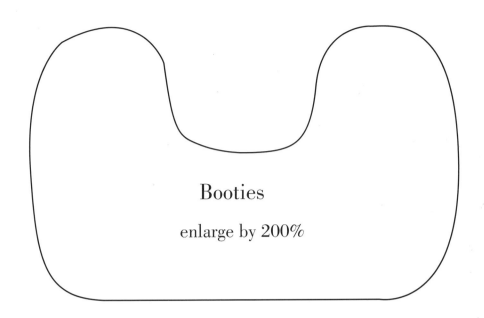

Booties

enlarge by 200%

 # Quick Appliqué Cushion, page 106–111

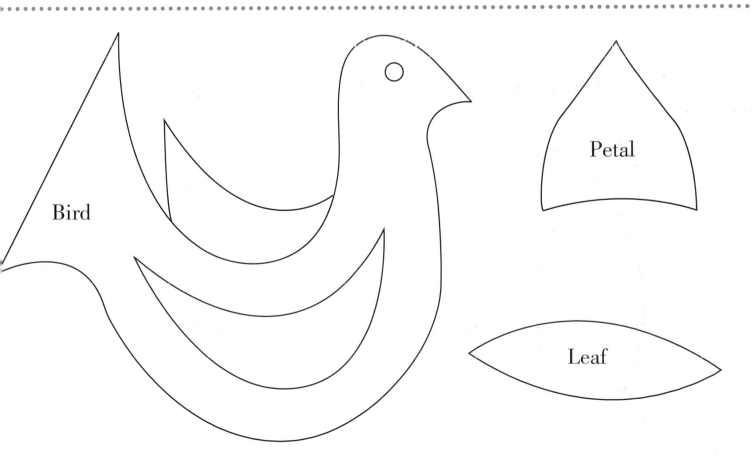

Bird

Petal

Leaf

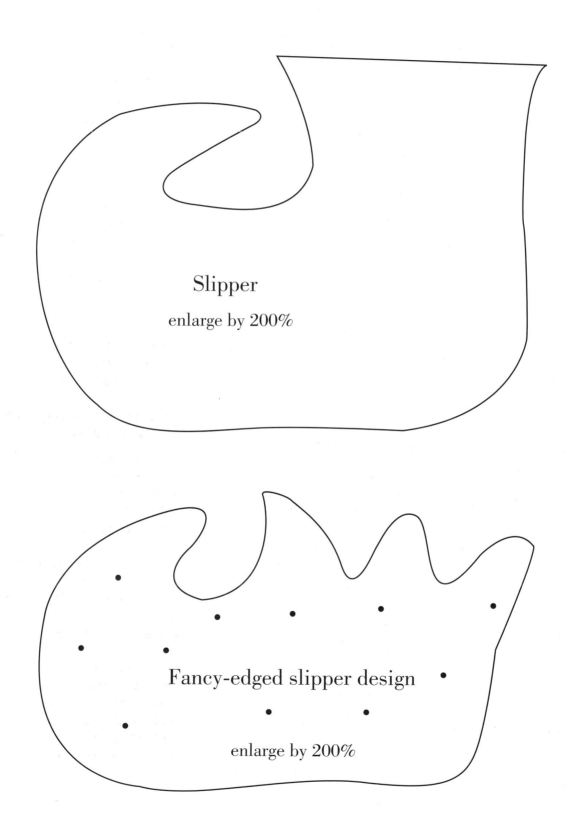

Slipper

enlarge by 200%

Fancy-edged slipper design

enlarge by 200%

Suppliers

UK

For carded fleece, Angelina fibres and felting needles:

Craftynotions Ltd
Unit 2
Jessop Way
Newark NG24 2ER
Tel: 01636 700862
www.craftynotions.com
(export service to USA also available)

Moral Fibre
Church Farm Studios
Stanton Lacy
Ludlow SY8 2AE
Tel: 01584 856654
Email: info@moralfibre.uk.com

Wingham Wool Work
70 Main Street
Wentworth
Rotherham
South Yorkshire S62 7TN
Tel: 01226 742926
www.winghamwoolwork.co.uk
(export service to USA also available)

For mail order:

Panduro Hobby
Tel: 0870 242 2875
www.panduro.co.uk

For boxes at Efco:

Sinotex
Tel: 01737 245450
www.sinotex.co.uk/efco

For shisha mirrors and a wide variety of sequins:

Hobby Craft
Tel: 0800 027 2387
www.hobbycraft.co.uk

For shisha mirrors and a wide variety of embroidery cotton (floss), ribbons and sequins:

John Lewis Partnership
Tel: 08456 049 049
www.johnlewis.com

For vintage-style fabrics:

Cabbages And Roses
3 Langton Street
London SW10 OJL
Tel: 020 7352 7333 or 020 8672 7333
www.cabbagesandroses.com

For dyes:

Dylon International Ltd
Worsley Bridge Road
Lower Sydenham
London SE26 5HD
Tel: 020 8663 4801
www.dylon.co.uk

For synthetic felt:

Hardy & Hanson
Tel: 01924 462353
www.hardy-hanson.co.uk

For a wide variety of silver and gold jewellery findings and beads:

Kernocraft Rocks & Gems Ltd
Bolingey
Perranporth
Cornwall TR6 ODH
Tel: 01872 573888
Email: info@kernocraft.com
www.kernocraft.com

USA

For synthetic felt:

Central Shippee
46 Star Lake Road
Bloomingdale NJ 07403
Tel: 973 838 1100
www.centralshippee.com

Distinctive Fabric
2023 Bay Street
Los Angeles CA 90021
Tel: 877 721 7269
www.distinctivefabric.com

J&O Fabrics
9401 Rt.130
Pennsauken NJ 08110
Tel: 856 663 2121
www.jandofabrics.com

For carded fleece, felting needles and Angelina fibres:

ABC Ranch Naturals
15249 Highway 19
Martinsburg
MO 65264
www.abcranch.com

New England Felting Supply Retail Store
84 Cottage Street
East Hampton MA 01027
Tel: 413 527 1188
www.feltingsupply.com

Suzanne Pufpaff
The Yurt Boutique
5038 East Quimby Road
Nashville MI 4973
Tel: 517 852 1871
www.yurtboutique.com

Acknowledgments

Many thanks to the following companies for so generously supplying materials for the book: Panduro Hobby, Dylon International, Kernocraft, John Lewis Partnership, Cabbages And Roses, Hobby Craft, Efco/Sinotex, Craftynotions and Wingham Wool Work.

Many thanks to Cheryl, Beth, Sarah, Pru and Mia for all of their hard work and experience, to Karl Adamson and Kim Sayer for their great photography and to Jo Richardson and Betsy Hosegood for all of their diligent and clever editing.

Finally, a big thank you to Chris and Rohan for putting up with wool fibres in their soup for months, and to Rachel and Terry Gill who make all things possible.

About the Author

Ellen Kharade is a professional writer and crafts person. She trained in Architectural Stained Glass and has worked for many years in glass conservation. Ellen has written several other books and is a regular contributor to *Crafts Beautiful* magazine. Ellen lives in Lincoln with her family.

Index